Panic Disorder

The Great Pretender

Panic Disorder

The Great Pretender

H. Michael Zal, D.O., F.A.C.N.

Clinical Professor, Department of Psychiatry
Philadelphia College of Osteopathic Medicine
Philadelphia, Pennsylvania
and
Chairman, Psychiatric Service
Metropolitan Hospital—Central Division
Philadelphia, Pennsylvania

Foreword by
Karl Rickels, M.D.

INSIGHT BOOKS

PLENUM PRESS • NEW YORK AND LONDON

Library of Congress Cataloging-in-Publication Data

Zal, H. Michael.
    Panic disorder : the great pretender / H. Michael Zal ; foreword
  by Karl Rickels.
        p.   cm.
    "Insight books."
    Includes bibliographical references.
    ISBN 0-306-43297-8
    1. Panic disorders. 2. Panic disorders--Treatment.   I. Title.
    [DNLM: 1. Anxiety Disorders. 2. Fear.   WM 178 Z22p]
  RC535.Z35   1989
  616.85'223--dc20
  DNLM/DLC
  for Library of Congress   89-23176
                                                                CIP

© 1990 Plenum Press, New York
A Division of Plenum Publishing Corporation
233 Spring Street, New York, N.Y. 10013

An Insight Book

Printed in the United States of America

TO

ALICE, MICHELLE, & FRED
whose love nourishes and sustains me

Foreword

While the 1970s was the decade of affective disorders, the 1980s can be considered the decade of anxiety disorders. For many years, anxiety disorders have been the stepchild of systematic research. Only more recently have surveys and epidemiological studies focused on anxiety and panic disorders to confirm that anxiety is frequently of a chronic nature, waxing and waning over a lifetime. Indeed, severe anxiety and panic are disabling illnesses that ultimately disrupt family, social, and work relationships.

Treatment of the anxiety disorders has been, for many years, the province of the psychoanalyst and the psychoanalytically oriented psychotherapist or counselor. While these psychological treatments may represent appropriate ways of dealing with the patient's anxiety, they have been rather unsuccessful in the management of patients with panic disorder, particularly when this condition was associated with phobic avoidance behavior. Furthermore, even behavioral approaches have left much to be desired as a singular treatment for these emotional problems.

With the recognition of panic disorder as a distinct subtype of anxiety, a search for more specific treatments began and was maintained primarily by biological psychiatrists. While the psychoanalytically oriented psychotherapist could be accused of bias in seeing all anxiety symptoms only as reactive and related to early childhood experiences and the unconscious, biological psychiatrists frequently became just as rigid, viewing panic disorder as "endogenous," occurring without apparent reason, not psychologically determined, and therefore to be treated only with drugs.

Now comes Dr. Zal, who subscribes to an integrative approach for the treatment of anxiety and panic. He makes the point that patients are not merely objects to be treated with medicines dispensed from a practitioner's black box or through a vending machine. Rather, they are human beings whose anxiety and panic have clear psychological determinants that require both drugs and psychotherapeutic intervention. Dr. Zal's holistic approach to the diagnosis and treatment of patients suffering from anxiety and/or panic disorder convincingly conveys to the reader that every suffering patient is a unique individual crying out for help; therefore, the best treatment of such a patient would most likely involve an approach that combines psychodynamic understanding, cognitive restructuring, and psychopharmacology.

It was a great pleasure for me to have been asked to write a foreword for this excellent book. I have known Dr. Zal professionally for over 10 years and have come to admire him as a clinician, teacher, and researcher. I consider the reading of this book a "must" not only for all mental health professionals and family physicians who deal with patients suffering from anxiety and/or panic but also for the many anxious patients who will learn more about their always painful, often disabling disease.

KARL RICKELS, M.D.

Stuart and Emily B. H. Mudd
Professor of Human Behavior
and Professor of Psychiatry,
The University of Pennsylvania

Chief Investigator,
University of Pennsylvania
Private Practice Research Group

Acknowledgments

It takes a long time from conception to the delivery of the final draft of a book. Some days are frustrating and raise new complications, through which the author has to push on. Along the road to publication of this book, there have been a number of wonderful people who have helped and encouraged me.

I am very appreciative to Howard P. Rome, M.D., Editorial Director, for his complimentary response and thoughtful editorial suggestions that helped me edit my lengthy essay, "Panic Disorder: Is It Emotional Or Physical?" for subsequent publication in *Psychiatric Annals*. It was with great happiness for myself and for the attention to the topic that I later accepted the 1988 Eric W. Martin Memorial Award for this article from the American Medical Writers Association. My thanks to Chairperson Art Gertel and the other members of the Martin Award Committee.

Special thanks to Karl Rickels, M.D. for agreeing to write the Foreword to this book but, more importantly, for his professional friendship over the last ten years.

I am also grateful to the following publishers for allowing me to reprint my work first published in their journals:

Slack Incorporated for Panic disorder: Is it emotional or physical? (*Psychiatric Annals*, 1987:177: 497–505), which appears as Chapter 5. It has been updated with reference to genetic linkages, and the section "Relationship to depression" has been deleted to avoid repetition; and From anxiety to panic disorder: A historical perspective (*Psychiatric Annals*, 1988:18:6:367–371), which, with a new introduction and some editorial changes, appears as Chapter 2.
Professional Marketing Systems, Inc., for Panic disorder: A special anxiety state (*Journal of Osteopathic Medicine*, 1988:2:9:41–50). This title and a portion of the text appear in Chapter 3.

Timeliness of topic and writing ability are not the only two prerequisites to having a book published. One has to find an editor who believes in the work and will consider it for publication. Such a person was Norma Fox, then editor-in-chief at Human Sciences Press. I am extremely thankful for her initial faith in my material that produced a contract in July of 1988. I am even more thankful that she remembered and followed through, after merger with Plenum Publishing Corporation, in her new position as executive editor. She and her editorial assistant, Frank Darmstadt, have been invaluable in allowing me to meet my deadlines. It has been a pleasure working with Herman Makler, senior production editor.

A special note of thanks is due my patients. During my twenty years in the practice of psychiatry, they have given me their respect and their trust. They have shared their problems and feelings with me in an open manner. I have gained great pleasure in seeing many of them improve and grow during our time together. The clinical vignettes in this book, although created out of the author's head, come partially out of this experience. In the few instances where direct material was used, I have of course disguised the people and situations involved.

I also appreciate the many people from all over the United States, Canada, Mexico, and Europe who requested reprints of my journal articles on panic disorder. Particularly memorable is a young woman who called to tell me that she could see herself in my article and was going to take it to her physician. Spreading awareness and treatment information is what this work is all about.

Emerson said: "A friend is a person with whom I may be sincere. Before him, I may think aloud." Fellow authors Sheila Weinstein and Carol Toussie Weingarten, R.N., Ph.D., certainly fulfill this definition for me. My thanks to them for their empathetic support during various stages of this book.

Finally, a word about my family. At the time of this writing, my wife, Alice, was a senior medical student at the Philadelphia College of Osteopathic Medicine. We had just celebrated our twenty-fourth wedding anniversary. Our daughter, Michelle, had just graduated from Boston University and is working as a graduate nurse. Our son, Fredrick, was a high school senior applying to college. Special thanks to him for "bugging" me to buy a personal computer and for helping me when I ran into trouble understanding its workings. Their achievements and affection nourish and sustain me. It is with pride and love that I have dedicated this book to them.

H. MICHAEL ZAL

Bala Cynwyd, Pennsylvania

Contents

15

Introduction

After many years of diagnostic confusion and untreated emotional pain, help is now available for those who suffer from panic disorder, a common but complex anxiety disorder.

Although a significant psychological problem, seen frequently in clinical practice, panic disorder remained unidentified until 1980. In that year, the American Psychiatric Association took a giant step in listing this cluster of emotional and physical symptoms as a distinct diagnostic category with definite diagnostic criteria. This has been an aid to quicker, more accurate diagnosis. Substantial research into its etiology and pathophysiology has produced new biological clues and instigated more appropriate treatment for this widespread emotional problem.

Panic attacks come on suddenly and intensely out of the blue. Feeling apprehensive and anxious, the patient fears dying, going crazy, or losing control. During an attack, these individuals also experience multiple distressing physical symptoms, such as shortness of breath, chest pain, palpitations, choking or smothering sensations, dizziness, gastrointestinal symptoms, hot and cold flashes, sweating and trembling. Some have a feeling of impending doom.

People often seek medical attention during and after these attacks. The "Great Pretender" is difficult to diagnose because it may mimic many physical diseases and show different confusing physical symptoms. Sometimes these physical symptoms present as "limited symptom attacks," which can add to the confusion. Many times, in spite of a thorough physical workup, no obvious cause is found.

Panic disorder can be disabling and interfere with the quality of life. Fearing that they will have an attack, people often develop secondary avoidance behavior and start to limit their life-style, staying home from work and away from social situations.

In spite of new information and increased public education, few laymen, physicians, or even mental health professionals are aware of the vicissitudes or the potential for successful treatment of panic disorder. For many, it is still confused with secondary phobic avoidance behavior, particularly agoraphobia. Few realize that panic disorder is usually primary. Many suffer silently, not understanding their painful and limiting disability.

Although many articles on various aspects of panic disorder have appeared in medical and psychiatric journals during the last ten years, very little is available in professional texts or books for the lay public. A review of psychiatric texts show only a few scattered paragraphs on panic disorder. The *Subject Guide to Books in Print* lists only a minimal number of titles involving panic disorder. At the time of my initial research, none of these were carried by the Free Library of Philadelphia or its suburban branches. They could not be found in local bookstores. Most of the available titles emphasized phobias and took a behavioral approach. None were written by a physician or a psychiatrist. None took a psychiatric, medical, or biological approach to panic disorder.

The hope is that this book will fill this void. It introduces panic disorder within the framework of anxiety. It provides an overview of etiological theories, diagnostic information, and treatment modalities. Although emphasizing a neuropsychiatric perspective, its orientation is holistic. In panic disorder, psychosocial and biological factors have an extraordinary relationship. Clinical research is slowing moving toward a synthesis of psychological, behavioral, and biological forces in understanding panic disorder. Our treatment preference involves an individualized treatment plan including reassurance, education, chemotherapy, and individual psychotherapy. It is a psychiatric approach that works.

Although written for the physician, psychiatrist, and mental health worker, this book will also appeal to general readers who want to educate themselves about panic disorder. Its aim is to disseminate new research information, foster an understanding of the clinical aspects of panic disorder, and create an awareness of new successful treatment methods. Perhaps this new knowledge will enable some of the undiagnosed multitude who suffer from panic disorder, the emotional problem of the 1980s, to come out of hiding and once again lead full productive lives.

1

Anxiety
Past, Present, and Future—A Question of Definition

Clinical Vignette: Mary Ann

Mary Ann was 53 years old. She was generally known as "high-strung" and had been "nervous" all her life. She tended to have trouble relaxing, was often restless, and felt shaky inside. She worried a lot, particularly about her children, finances, and about how others saw her.

She was a hard and conscientious worker. She had always felt better if she was active and busy. As darkness fell, it seemed harder to avoid her problems and keep her feelings in check. She thus had trouble falling asleep at times. She knew that when she was tense and under stress, the muscles of her neck contracted, and she had terrible headaches.

Mary Ann was also prone to gastrointestinal ailments, such as indigestion, nausea, and diarrhea. When feeling overwhelmed, her physical and emotional symptoms escalated and she experienced a vague feeling that something terrible was going to happen. Frustrated and alone, she feared going crazy or losing control.

At times of crisis, she often looked to her physician to explain her distress. She tended to vacillate between her family doctor and her gynecologist. Usually, neither physician could find any obvious physical cause for her debilitating complaints. They realized that her ailments were symptomatic of anxiety, but neither could offer more than passing emotional support and an occasional prescription for a minor tranquilizer or sleeping pill. Their office staffs were often given the chore of taking her multiple calls. It is not surprising that her primary physicians were perplexed and frustrated by her symptoms.

Anxiety is a universal feeling. We have all experienced the uncomfortable subjective emotional and

25

bodily changes that reflect its presence. However, it is often difficult to understand, tolerate, and accept when it is happening to others. Like its Latin original, *anxietas*, anxiety commonly connotes an experience of varying blends of uncertainty, agitation, and dread. These feelings can be transmitted to others and make them feel tense and ill at ease. No one can escape its presence in their own lives. No one who works with people can avoid it in clinical practice. Nevertheless, anxiety is often a puzzle to the physician as well as to other members of the helping professions.

The human mind has many ways of conceptualizing and communicating this feeling. Patients use many emotional and somatic terms to describe their suffering. They say they are nervous, uneasy, troubled, upset, scared, restless, and worried. They complain of feeling tense in their muscles or of a funny feeling in the pit of their stomach. They report troubled and symbolic dreams. They become irritable and less cooperative. These messages of distress, often signaling mental and/or physical illness, have gone through many changes in interpretation. It is not surprising that even the professionals are confused.

It is only during the last hundred years that psychiatry has started to understand anxiety and its various ramifications. And it is only during the last decade that its nuances have started to be clarified. The inclusion during this time of panic disorder and posttraumatic stress disorder within the categories of anxiety disorder has further broadened its meaning. Its clinical aspects and characteristic features continue to grow. Avoidance behavior, for instance, is now often emphasized. Various bodily organ systems, gastrointestinal, cardiovascular, and respiratory, are coming under closer scrutiny as carriers of "masked" anxiety. However, a clear definition of anxiety that is clinically helpful is still evolving. Perhaps looking back will help us look forward and enable us to better define anxiety and better diagnose patients such as Mary Ann.

History

During the last decade, the study of anxiety has become one of the fastest growing areas of research in psychiatry and neurobiology. This has not always been so. Unlike depression, which had been described for centuries, anxiety did not come to the fore until the second half of the nineteenth century. In fact, it all started with DaCosta and the publication of his article "On Irritable Heart . . ." in 1871 in the *American Journal of Medical Sciences*.[1] Anxiety has stalked through the last 100 years under a whole rogues' gallery of aliases. This functional syndrome, describing the cardiac manifestations of anxiety, has taken on a bewildering number of diagnostic labels which seem to be related to, and to change following each major war:

Cardiac neurosis
Effort syndrome (World War I)
Soldier's heart
Neurocirculatory asthenia (World War I)
Nervous exhaustion
Vasomotor neurosis
Aviator's syndrome
Anxiety state (World War II)

"As the majority of the terms suggest, the somatic side of pathological anxiety has repeatedly captured the attention of earlier clinical investigators."[2]

However, this is not the whole picture. The term anxiety is used in a variety of ways, depending on the author's perspective. A more exact definition must also take other dimensions into account. As we saw in our clinical vignette of Mary Ann, a subjective approach tells us that although anxiety is widespread, it is a non-specific symptom that is uniquely individualized. Philosophical hypotheses can add additional shades of meaning but are out of the scope of this book. Psychological, behavioral, and physiological viewpoints will be briefly examined in the hope of developing a more exact definition of anxiety.

Theories of Anxiety

Even within the field of psychology and psychiatry, there are different viewpoints. "In Freud's hands, DaCosta's syndrome was turned inside out. Anxiety was brought from behind the physical symptoms that for DaCosta and his followers constituted the whole of the disorder, and was then seen to be the central unifying factor that organized and gave collective form to the somatic manifestations."[2]

To a psychoanalyst, anxiety is of crucial theoretical importance. Freud saw anxiety as a signal of danger which plays a central role in the functioning of the psychic apparatus. The ego reacts to an internal threat arising from the id (forbidden drives) by experiencing mental pain (anxiety) in consciousness. The pain causes the ego to use certain defense mechanisms to try to control the drives. In this sense, "neurotic anxiety" is a signal that certain unacceptable impulses (sexual or aggressive) are trying to break into consciousness.

In 1923, Otto Rank, the founder of "will" therapy, started to interpret Freudian concepts in terms of the trauma of birth. He was the first of a long line of therapists who view the separation of the child from symbiosis with the mother as the most traumatic experience in the human condition and the root of "primal anxiety." This was thought to be the basis of all subsequent "separation anxiety." His "will" therapy helped the patient reexperience the birth trauma.

Psychologist Rollo May accepted Freud's ideas but added to them from existentialism. The existential philosophers believe that anxiety is a specific human way of existence. Kierkegaard, the founder of existentialism, is credited with first describing anxiety in his 1844 book, *The Concept of Dread.* He believed that the freedom to choose with no guarantees of the correct choice caused dread and anxiety. He felt that anxiety was intrinsic to the human condition. The more choices, the more anxiety.

Although other existentialists, such as Jaspers, Heidegger, and Sartre, differed on the question of belief in God, they agreed that "man is free to make choices and that freedom is the source of his anxiety."[3] In his 1950 book, *The Meaning of Anxiety,* Rollo May calls anxiety "a nameless and formless uneasiness that has dogged the footsteps of modern man." As he further defines it: "Anxiety is the apprehension cued off by a threat to some value that the individual holds essential to his existence as a personality."[4]

In contrast to Freud's belief that psychic anxiety was primary and led to the development of physical symptoms, stands psychologist William James's proposal that the physical experience is primary. He regarded the psychological experience of anxiety as nothing more than an awareness of the physical symptoms of anxiety.

John B. Watson, the father of behaviorism, rejected Freud's theories. In 1920, he described a study of "Little Albert,"[5] demonstrating the importance of Pavlovian or "classical" conditioning and stimulus generalization in the development of phobic reactions. Learning theory tells us that fears are conditioned responses, and thus learned. Some now explain certain anxiety reactions, especially panic attacks, as learned responses that are best understood in terms of behavioral mechanisms.

B. F. Skinner coined the term "operant conditioning." Here the subject learns to "operate" in ways calculated to produce pleasure or avoid pain. Joseph Volpe in 1952 defined anxiety along these parameters. "Anxiety is the automatic response pattern characteristic of a particular individual organism after the administration of a noxious stimulus."[6]

This historical overview of the path that anxiety has taken in the last 100 or so years, and some of the theories of anxiety popular during that time, may have broadened your concept of the meaning of anxiety. However, you probably still do not feel that you have all the tools comfortably to diagnose anxiety in that patient sitting before you. A through clinical understanding that will have more practical applications requires that we look at additional issues.

A Physiologic Viewpoint

To fully define anxiety, we first have to understand the emotion of fear and the physiologic perspective.

"Fear is one of the four basic and universal (primary) emotional states (along with joy, sorrow, and anger). Normal fear consists of subjective apprehension and objective physiologic changes, both of which are appropriate in degree and duration to a consciously recognized external danger. It involves recognition and arousal, with preparation for action . . . (i.e., fight or flight). Fear dissipates in proportion to the perceived reduction in the intensity of danger."[7] Both fear and anxiety are signals warning of impending danger which enable the person to take measures to deal with a threat. Anxiety is *dis-junctive* a response to unknown danger, usually warns of an internal danger or conflict, and is unequal to the danger involved. Fear, on the other hand, signals a real external danger and is *equal* to that danger.

Understanding the objective physiologic changes seen with fear will help us comprehend the physical symptoms of anxiety. In 1916, Walter B. Cannon,[8] a Harvard physiologist, first described the bodily changes that occur in response to danger or threat. These physiologic responses are designed to prepare the organism for emergency action at the expense of digestion and other visceral functions. He believed that anxiety began in the brain. He noted that when the cortex of the brain perceives a threat, it sends a stimulus down the sympathetic branch of the autonomic nervous system to the adrenal glands. Under the influence of epinephrine, various changes mediated by the autonomic nervous system are seen.

Respiration deepens (rapid respiration with hyperventilation), the heart beats more rapidly (tachycardia), the arterial pressure rises, and there is tremor of skeletal muscles. Blood is redistributed from skin and viscera (stomach and intestines) to the muscle tissue, central nervous system, and heart. The spleen contracts and discharges its store of corpuscles, which provide for essential oxygen and for riddance of acid waste. All these changes serve to render the body more effective in the violent display of energy that responses to danger demand.

Stimulation of the sympathetic nervous system can also produce pupil dilatation, cold sweats with clammy palms, pallor, and piloerection. We know that the parasympathetic nervous system is also involved in our autonomic response to danger. This explains why such effects as increased frequency of urination, emptying of the rectum (diarrhea), slowing of the heart rate, nausea ("butterflies" in the stomach), vomiting, and lowered blood pressure can also be seen.

Thus, understanding the subjective and objective symptoms of fear enables us to better comprehend the emotional and physical components of anxiety. Anxiety is similar to fear in its somatic or bodily accompaniment. It is different from fear in that "it is a response to a frightening inner impulse rather than to an external danger, and it has a central quality of eerie dread. In some individuals, the dread may have a specific content (that one is dying of a heart attack, for example); in others it may be a nameless terror."[9]

Normal versus Abnormal Anxiety

Although many people experience anxiety, sometimes every day, there is often a quantitative difference in their complaints. It is important for the physician or mental health professional to recognize the difference between pathological anxiety and anxiety as a normal or adaptive response. However, regardless of our skill in differential diagnosis, it is a difficult clinical judgment to determine where normal anxiety ends and abnormal anxiety begins.

Anxiety is the central or associated feature of most psychiatric illnesses. In the anxiety disorders, it is the predominant or sole manifestation of illness. Here it may be expressed directly as a subjective emotion associated with a variety of physical symptoms, such as is seen in generalized anxiety disorder or panic disorder, or controlled unconsciously by the production of phobias, obsessive-compulsive, or dissociative symptoms. As an associated symptom, it is seen in psychotic disorders, eating disorders, and depressive disorders.

Anxiety can also be caused by or associated with physical pathology. It is a component of many physical illnesses, but can also be confused with primary physical disease. Unadaptive anxiety can result from vitamin B1 deficiency (beriberi), hypoglycemic syndrome, hyperthyroidism, adrenal tumors (pheochromocytoma), and temporal lobe seizures. Ménière's disease may be mistakenly diagnosed as an anxiety disorder. Other causes of anxiety of organic origin include caffeine or amphetamine intoxication and drug and alcohol withdrawal.

"Finally, the symptoms of anxiety, especially in the dramatic form of a panic attack that drives the patient to an emergency ward for help, may be mistaken for an acute myocardial infarction. More than one patient who has been rushed to a cardiac intensive care unit has been found in course of an extended and careful study of the coronary circulation to have no abnormalities other than panic disorder."[9]

The Positive Aspects of Anxiety

Some believe that "nobody needs or wants anxiety." They feel that it is "an undesirable emotion" that
"leads to nothing useful . . ."[3] However, in moderate
degree, anxiety can be termed "normal" and has various positive aspects. It can serve as a constructive force,
increasing alertness and effort. Levels of anxiety within
the individual's capacity to cope with it are conducive to
learning and growth.

"Anxiety responses conditioned to stimulus situations objectively associated with danger are judged
adaptive."[6] It often serves a useful purpose in prepar-
ing a person for a potentially threatening or serious situation, such as an exam, speech, or battle. "It builds
character, enhances creativity, enlarges awareness of
life's possibilities . . . keeps us on our social toes. Crim-
inals commit crimes because they don't have anxiety."[3]

"Under certain circumstances a low degree of anxiety may enhance such functions as performing on stage
(The Yerkes-Dodson Law)."[6] "In addition, anxiety is
frequently a strong motivating force in decision making,
its unpleasantness pushing the individual toward the
resolution of some inhibiting impasse caused by internal conflicts."[10] "The role of anxiety is particularly
prominent in individual character formation and personality development. The uneasiness and apprehension aroused by the disapproval of parents, for instance, often brings about constructive changes in a
child's behavior."[11]

In a panel discussion on anxiety,[12] Thomas P.
Hackett, M.D., points out another situation in which
anxiety is desirable. "We know through Irving Janis's
work that a little preoperative anxiety is good for the

postoperative condition, making postoperative depression less likely. . . I think that not only psychologic morbidity, but also physical morbidity is lowered in individuals who have 'appropriate' anxiety before surgery. . . From the lay press, one would get the idea that anxiety is not only unnecessary, but also bad, and yet we know that isn't true. It's a hard thing to convince someone to learn to control or live with, because basically it's an unpleasant state of mind, and so many people think that unmitigated happiness is the ideal."

Sidney Cohen, M.D., another panelist, continues this train of thought. "It is the unpleasant aspects of living from which we learn to cope, to deal with frustrating events, and therefore we have to educate individuals that being in a constant state of euphoria or pleasure is not a desirable way of life. . . ." Every patient who walks into your office complaining of anxiety does not have to be silenced with medication. Explanation and reassurance may be all that is needed to calm the patient and facilitate growth.

Pathological Anxiety

Pathological or unadaptive anxiety is more severe, intense, and pervasive. Rickels and Schweizer define it as follows. "If it is intense enough, persistent enough, or out of proportion to any known life circumstance, then it probably qualifies as abnormal."[13] An abnormal or unhealthy degree of anxiety is reached when a person's ability to deal with the stress-producing situation is exceeded. In our introductory vignette, Mary Ann had reached this point.

"If the level [of anxiety] is considerable, it interferes

with the effective performance of many classes of behavior. The generalized rise in muscle tension impairs
coordination of movement. Mental concentration, the
ready flow of associations, and the registration of im-
pressions may all be diminished. (This leads many patients to feel that they are getting senile.) There may be
reduced efficiency at work, impaired social functioning,
or inadequate sexual behavior—manifested as impo-
tence in males and frigidity in females."[6]

Two to five percent of the total population experience a clinically significant anxiety state at some time in
their life. "A recent study by the National Institute of
Mental Health found that more than 13 million Americans suffer from these disorders."[3] When the severity of
the anxiety bears little relationship to the situation, consistently interferes with the capacity to experience satis-
faction or pleasure, or restricts normal activity, it can
certainly be considered pathological. At this point, it is
time to seek professional help.

The Signs and Symptoms of Anxiety

As you can see, "mental and bodily functions find
in anxiety a meeting place that is unparalleled in other
aspects of human life."[2] To understand anxiety fully, it
is important to look at both its emotional and physical
aspects. An understanding of this dyad will be even
more important when we move on to the discussion of
panic disorder.

The mixture of physical and psychological symptoms characteristic of anxiety are hard to miss in the
extreme. However, much variation and combination are
seen as we move along the continuum of the anxiety

disorders. Although the combination of experiences that constitute the anxiety response varies greatly from one individual to another, it is quite consistent within individuals. Characteristic patterns can thus be recognized. It is easier to observe these patterns if we are aware of the components that may show themselves. The following is a summary of the various signs and symptoms of anxiety that may be involved.

Emotional or Mental Aspects of Anxiety (Psychic Anxiety)

   Feeling tense or keyed up ✓
   Irritability ✓
   Suddenly scared for no reason ✓
   Fears of heights, darkness, or being alone ✓
   Social fears ✓
   Sexual worries ✓
   Fear of death ✓
   Nervous or shaky inside ✓
   Spells of terror or panic ✓

Physiological Aspects of Anxiety (Somatic Anxiety)

Cardiovascular
   Palpitations ✓
   Dizziness
   Faintness
   Chest pain ✓

Respiratory
   Shortness of breath ✓
   Hyperventilation

Muscular
   Trembling
   Shaking ✓
   Weakness ✓

Gastrointestinal
   Indigestion ✓
   Nausea and vomiting
   Butterflies in stomach ✓
   Diarrhea
   Flatulence

Other
   Sweating ✓
   Headache ✓
   Constant urge to urinate ✓
   Feeling restless and having difficulty sitting still ✓

A Modern View

In spite of the other psychological and behavioral viewpoints noted here, Freud's opinion that psychic anxiety was primary and led to the development of physical symptoms dominated psychiatric nosology until the publication of the third edition of the *Diagnostic and Statistical Manual of Mental Disorders* (DSM-III)[14] in 1980. This manual documents a change from a Freudian to a more descriptive approach in classification. This was considered revolutionary in psychiatry. In the next chapter, we shall take a closer look at the evolution of this new classification and its ramifications.

During the last decade, the perspective has turned around and we are again being asked to evaluate our patients from a more descriptive, empirical, and somatic point of view, rather than from the dynamic, analytic (Freudian) vantage point. The psychoanalytic viewpoint is being eclipsed even more by biologic and psychopharmacological research in all areas that has tended to carry us farther down the neurochemical, neurophysiological, and biogenetic pathways to understanding anxiety. A more pragmatic approach to mental illness is evolving in American psychiatry.

Here anxiety is seen as an imbalance of the benzodiazepine-GABA receptor complex. Since the advent of using a brain imaging technique called positron emission tomography (PET scan), the spotlight has been on neurophysiology and brain chemistry. Abnormalities have been found that are believed to determine vulnerability to anxiety attacks.[15] If these abnormalities are persistent, they could be evaluated as genetic markers.

The focus of the future is on this psychobiologic orientation. Because of this view, a new approach to anxious patients is being taken. Anxiety is no longer seen as a single entity but rather as several discrete conditions or illnesses. These include panic disorder, posttraumatic stress disorder, generalized anxiety disorder, phobias, and obsessive-compulsive disorder. This new awareness is efficient clinically and has had its effects on classification, diagnosis, and treatment. It would have taken Mary Ann some time in classical psychoanalysis to realize that her symptoms of distress did have meaning and were a signal of anxiety. It would have taken even longer to "cure" her or make her feel more comfortable. Today, her case can be diagnosed and treated in a much shorter period of time.

Anxiety is an enigma. Its exact definition remains elusive due to the fact that it is used in a variety of ways depending on the author's perspective. It is thus often a

puzzle to the physician as well as to the layman. This
chapter reviews the history of the clinical entity. Beginning with DaCosta in 1871, it was initially viewed from
a somatic or physical vantage point. However, due to
Freud's work, anxiety was turned inside out and
viewed from a dynamic or analytic perspective. During
the last decade, since the publication of the DSM-III, we
are again asked to view anxiety in a more descriptive,
empirical, and somatic way.

Subjective, philosophical, psychological, behavioral, and physiological viewpoints, which add nuances
to the definition of anxiety, were also reviewed. The
relationship of fear to anxiety, normal versus abnormal
anxiety, and the positive aspects of anxiety were explained. The signs and symptoms of anxiety were enumerated. These physical and emotional signs and
symptoms are now considered the pieces that have to
be put together to more clearly define, diagnose, and
treat the puzzle of anxiety. The modern view places the
spotlight on neurochemical dimensions and brain abnormalities. The focus of the future is on this psychobiologic orientation. This chapter, by pulling together
some of the historical, theoretical, and clinical aspects of
anxiety, will help you to better look for and understand
this symptom complex as it presents itself. Comprehen-
sion of this information is critical to understanding our
later discussion of the vicissitudes of panic disorder.

2

From Anxiety to Panic Disorder
An Historical Perspective

It was not until 1980 that panic disorder had a name. Prior to this time, millions of its sufferers were seen less clearly as part of the overall category of generalized anxiety disorders. How could such an important entity have taken so long to come out of the shadows into the light? Although anxiety is ageless and may even be, as Pascal said, the state of man,[1] as an aspect of mental illness it has gone through many changes in interpretation. It is only during the twentieth century that it has been clearly defined, classified, and understood. Its clinical ramifications and classification continue to evolve. Even as recently as 1987, the American Psychiatric Association made still further adjustments in its classification.

In the last ten years, panic disorder, its latest family member, has come to the fore as one of the most studied of the anxiety disorders. The physician can only correctly treat that which he knows. As we shall see, this new perspective has ultimately affected treatment considerations. Many patients are now being helped for the first time. The new classification system that prompted its emergence as a separate diagnostic category represented a definite shift in diagnostic thinking in the field of psychiatry. Let us look at some of the historical background that led up to this revolutionary change and admitted panic disorder as the newest member of the anxiety family.

The Classification of Mental Disorders

The first stage of understanding in any science is classification. This is equally true in psychiatry. The federal government has collected and published statistical data on the mentally ill in the United States since the decennial census of 1840. In that census, the idiotic and insane were enumerated as a single class; no distinction was made between the two categories. It was not until 1880 that an attempt was made to classify the mentally ill in the United States by type of mental disorder. The classification of mental disorders used in the special census of patients in mental hospitals in 1923 was used with only minor modifications until 1934. In that year, it was revised to conform to the more extensive classification of mental diseases contained in the first edition of the *Standard Nomenclature of Diseases* (Jordan, 1933). This classification served as the basis for the collection of statistics on the diagnostic characteristics of patients admitted to mental hospitals in the United States until the publication, in 1952, of the first edition of the *Diagnostic and Statistical Manual* (DSM-I), by the American Psychiatric Association.

1952—*Diagnostic and Statistical Manual* (DSM-I)

The DSM-I was greatly influenced by the theories of an Austrian neurologist, Sigmund Freud, the founder of psychoanalysis. In his writings, he deals with the concept of anxiety,[2] calling it *Angst*, which in German denotes a more intense feeling than the English word. Initially, Freud considered anxiety the outcome of repressed sexuality (libido). He later replaced this notion with the broader conception of anxiety as a signal of danger. He distinguishes between objective (real) anxiety (fear) and neurotic anxiety. "In psychoanalytic theory, anxiety is differentiated from fear. Anxiety is the person's response to a danger that threatens from within in the form of a forbidden instinctual drive, that is about to escape from his control. Fear, on the other hand, is defined as the reaction to a real external danger that threatens the person with possible injury or death."[3]

In psychodynamic theory, anxiety is viewed as playing a central role in the functioning of the psychic apparatus. The personality is divided into three parts: the id, ego, and superego. The id is comprised of basic instinctual drives and operates on the pleasure principle. The ego describes the portion of the personality that deals with the external world. It is roughly synonymous with "self," or the "I" of personality. The superego represents a system of values and roughly represents the conscience.

The ego reacts to an internal threat arising from the id (forbidden drives) by experiencing mental pain (anxiety) in consciousness. The pain causes the ego to use certain defense mechanisms to try to control the drives. In this sense, anxiety is a signal that certain unacceptable impulses (sexual and aggressive) are trying to break into consciousness. The primary ego defense mechanism is repression, which tries to keep us unaware of the forbidden impulse or feeling. If repression does not work, the ego must call into play various auxiliary defenses or mental mechanisms. These include conversion, somatization, dreaming, fantasy, complex formation, condensation, symbolization, suppression, introjection, identification, displacement, aim inhibition, projection, reaction formation, undoing, sublimation, compensation, rationalization, idealization, isolation of affect, denial, and dissociation.[4]

The Freudian concept further divides anxiety into four categories, depending on the nature of the feared consequences, and the point of early psychosexual growth and development where the conflict arose. These include id or impulse anxiety (object loss), separation anxiety (loss of love), castration anxiety, and superego anxiety (guilt). "If the defenses are successful, the anxiety is dispelled or safely contained, but, depending on the nature of the defenses used, the person may develop a variety of neurotic symptoms."[3] This total theory came to form the basis of dynamic psychiatry.

The DSM-I presented a nosology based for the most part on this Freudian psychoanalytic worldview of anxiety as neurosis. It was not until 1948 that an International Classification of Mental Disorders—the ICD—became available. The ICD had its origin in the International Classification of Causes of Death, which was adopted by the International Statistical Institute in Paris in 1893. However, the classification of mental disorders in ICD was unsatisfactory for classifying many of the diagnostic terms that were introduced in the DSM-I. An international collaborative effort was started in 1957 to rectify this problem and culminated in the International Revision Conference of July, 1965.

1968—DSM-II

The second edition of the *Diagnostic and Statistical Manual* (DSM-II) was published in 1968 and was based on the classification of mental disorders in the ICD-8, as approved by the World Health Organization in 1966. The new classification was considered an achievement of the first order in international professional collaboration, taking into account established knowledge of etiol-

TABLE 1 Neuroses, from the
Diagnostic and Statistical Manual
of Mental Disorders,
Second Edition (DSM-II)

Anxiety neurosis
Hysterical neurosis
Hysterical neurosis, conversion type
Hysterical neurosis, dissociative type
Phobic neurosis
Obsessive-compulsive neurosis
Depressive neurosis
Neurasthenic neurosis
Depersonalization neurosis
Hypochondriacal neurosis
Other neurosis

ogy. Where such knowledge is not available, it attempts to provide a middle ground to satisfy the needs of psychiatrists of different schools of theoretical orientation.[5]

In spite of the "middle ground" approach heralded in the introduction to the DSM-II, it, like its older sibling, the DSM-I, presented a classification based for the most part on the Freudian concept of anxiety as neurosis. It includes a large category of diagnosis under the title Neuroses (see Table 1). It thus takes a dynamic approach, indicating a particular etiologic process based on the Freudian view of "the development of maladaptive behavior and 'neurotic' symptoms as a consequence of defensive mechanisms operating to prevent conscious awareness of painful intrapsychic conflict."[6]

The ICD-9,[7] currently in widespread use in Europe, also takes a dynamic point of view. It uses the term "neurosis," and places all anxiety conditions under the category of anxiety states (see Table 2).

In DSM-II terminology, patients whom we now

TABLE 2   Neurotic Disorders
(Abridged), from the *International
Classification of Diseases,*
Ninth Edition (ICD-9)

Anxiety states
Hysteria
Phobic state
Obsessive-compulsive disorders
Neurotic depression
Neurasthenia
Depersonalization syndrome
Hypochondriasis
Other neurotic disorders
Acute reaction to stress
Adjustment reaction

know to be showing symptoms of a panic disorder
would probably have been diagnosed as having an anxiety neurosis. According the the ICD-9, they would
have an anxiety state. Most likely they would have
spent many months or years on a psychoanalytic couch
trying to understand the conflicts that led to their neurosis. At the other end of the therapeutic spectrum,
they may have been offered "supportive therapy."
They may have been given a barbiturate or, perhaps, in
the early 1950s, meprobamate. After 1961, and the advent of chlordiazepoxide (Librium), which ushered in
the era of benzodiazepines, they probably would have
been handed some form of a minor tranquilizer to "set-
tle their nerves," and sent on their way. Today, we look
at these cases differently in reference to diagnosis and
treatment.

TABLE 3   Classification of Anxiety Disorders, from the *Diagnostic and Statistical Manual of Mental Disorders*, Third Edition (DSM-III)

A. Phobic Disorders (Phobic Neurosis)
   1. Agoraphobia with panic attacks ✓
   2. Agoraphobia without panic attacks
   3. Social Phobia ✓
   4. Simple Phobia ✓

B. Anxiety States (Anxiety Neurosis)
   1. Panic Disorder ✓
   2. Generalized Anxiety Disorder ✓
   3. Obsessive-compulsive disorder (Obsessive-compulsive Neurosis) ✓

C. Post-Traumatic Stress Disorder
   1. Acute
   2. Chronic or delayed
   3. Atypical anxiety disorder

{ probably my father, and me, after my mother's death}

1980—DSM-III

The American Psychiatric Association took a giant and helpful step in 1980 when they published the third edition of the *Diagnostic and Statistical Manual of Mental Disorders* (DSM-III). Included therein was a reclassification of anxiety, and for the first time, panic disorder emerges as a separate diagnostic entity under the heading of Anxiety States (see Table 3).

This new classification system represented a definite shift in diagnostic thinking in psychiatry—a revolutionary change that would also affect treatment. For the first time, we were not dealing with the word "neurosis." The focus was no longer on psychoanalytic theory that defined neurotic syndromes as developing from the interplay of unconscious internal conflicts and the mental mechanisms of defense operating to prevent their emergence into consciousness.

Rather, we were asked to evaluate our patients from a more descriptive, empirical, and somatic point of view instead of from the dynamic, analytic (Freudian) vantage point. Anxiety was now seen as having both mental/psychic and somatic components. As we saw in Chapter 1, this new way of looking at anxiety and, particularly, panic disorder relies heavily on a more clinical understanding of the subjective emotional symptoms of anxiety and its objective physical or physiological signs.

The reasons for this decision apparently centered around treatment patterns and response. Panic, generalized anxiety, and phobias, although all showing anxiety as a central symptom, respond differently to various treatment modalities.

Desensitization, a form of behavioral therapy, is less effective in patients with episodes of panic and more helpful where phobia is the only symptom.

Pharmacological treatment also differs in patients with and without panic. Patients with panic disorder respond better to antidepressants and/or minor tranquilizers, while those with generalized anxiety disorder symptoms without panic attacks do better on minor tranquilizers. This was first identified by Sargant[7] in the case of monoamine oxidase inhibitors and by Klein[8] for tricyclic antidepressants.

Schweizer and Rickels offer two other speculative reasons for this change in classification in the DSM-III. "The introduction of chlorpromazine in 1954, and the rapid development of antidepressants and anxiolytics in subsequent years, not only offered the promise of chemical treatment of distressing emotional symptoms, it also and perhaps more importantly, stimulated the resurgence once again of an empirical and descriptive turn of mind. New drugs had to be tested on target populations to establish safety, and later, efficacy. To do this effectively, quantifiable rating scales had to be developed that could accurately track symptom improvement and side effect development . . . Diagnostic criteria became obligatory for entry into pharmacologic studies, and making empirical definition of clinical populations an accepted strategy. . . . Another impetus for this shift . . . was the growth of the insurance industry and its reimbursement for treatment of mental illness. It did not take long for the insurance industry to recognize the cost ineffectiveness of psychoanalytic-based treatments, and to provide disincentives for applying them."[9]

We wonder why the ICD-9, which went into effect in 1979, neglects to mention panic disorder. "Perhaps the ambiguity of the word anxiety and its failure to cross the language barriers of Europe without being misunderstood has hindered further inquiry."[10] This problem certainly was seen previously in Freud's use of the word *Angst* in his discussion of anxiety in *A General Introduction to Psychoanalysis*.

Classification Controversies

Controversy over the classification changes persist. Critics of the diagnostic separation wonder if panic disorder is really a persistent and independent disorder separate from other anxiety states. Differentiating between a panic disorder and generalized anxiety remains confusing for some. "When patients say they have been 'nervous' all their lives, they are usually talking about generalized anxiety. People with generalized anxiety disorder show fewer autonomic nervous system or physical symptoms and an earlier, more gradual, onset of anxiety.[11] In general, the intensity of their anxiety is less than in panic attacks. . . . According to the DSM-III-R, to be diagnosed as a generalized anxiety disorder a person must feel anxious (nervous, tense, or restless, feel on edge, or irritable) and have unrealistic or excessive worry about two or more life circumstances (often about misfortune to one's child or finances), on most days, for six months or longer. . . .[12] They may not, however, have specific attacks or have other symptoms, such as physical complaints, of panic disorder. Some patients with panic disorder may experience generalized anxiety between attacks."[11]

Others wonder if panic disorder is not indeed a variant of depressive disorder. "Because loss seems to be a recurrent theme in panic disorder, there are those who feel that it is simply another phase of depression. Longitudinal studies are needed to tell if panic disorder is a unique diagnostic entity or really an atypical depression and part of the spectrum of depressive illness. There is some evidence that patients with panic are likelier to have a greater family history of depressive illness than anxious patients without panic, suggesting a link with depressive disorder.

"In the small sample of patients seen in my private practice, I have noted a history of loss in those diagnosed as panic disorder. In that depression is often a reaction to loss, I was not surprised to also see symptoms of an underlying depression in many of these patients. Complicating the issue further is the fact that many panic disorder patients become secondarily depressed because of their frustration over the chronicity of their suffering and the limitations which their disorder has imposed on their life."[13]

Another area of controversy in classification has been the relationship between agoraphobia and panic *My father* disorder. Panic patients may compound their problem by gradually starting to avoid situations and places where they had an attack or fear that they will have an attack. For instance, they may not want to drive their car or go to the supermarket. These avoidance behaviors may escalate into the development of an actual phobia—a persistent and irrational fear which results in the avoidance of an object or situation to the point that it causes significant distress and interferes with their functioning. Thus, phobias can be a complication of panic disorder.

The most common associated phobia here is agoraphobia—a fear of being alone or in a public place from which it may be difficult to escape or get help in case of incapacitation. This may involve crowds, tunnels, bridges, elevators, or public transportation. The area of contention here that prolongs the controversy is, which comes first, panic disorder or agoraphobia?

Some see agoraphobia as a significant and frequent secondary manifestation of panic disorder. Others see it as primary. Further complications arise when patients seek help for their chronic disabling agoraphobia, forgetting completely their initial and thus primary panic symptoms. This point can be missed completely unless a thorough history is taken. This situation has prolonged the classification controversy as to which comes first, panic disorder or agoraphobia.

TABLE 4   Anxiety Disorders, from the
*Diagnostic and Statistical Manual
of Mental Disorders,*
Third Edition–Revised (DSM-III-R)

Panic disorder with agoraphobia
  Specify current severity of agoraphobic
  avoidance
  Specify current severity of panic attacks
Panic disorder without agoraphobia
  Specify current severity of panic attacks
Agoraphobia without history of panic disorder
  Specify with or without limited symptom
  attacks
Simple phobia
Obsessive-compulsive disorder
Post-traumatic stress disorder
  Specify if delayed onset
Generalized anxiety disorder
Anxiety disorder NOS

1987—DSM-III-R

The DSM-III-R,[12] published in May 1987, addresses this issue and presents a new arrangement of anxiety disorders (see Table 4). A comparison with the DSM-III (see Table 3) shows a reshuffling and dissolution of the three categories, with a new linear arrangement under the heading "Anxiety Disorders." Panic disorder is now designated as existing with or without agoraphobia.

"In the great majority of cases of 'agoraphobia' that are seen in clinical settings, the phobic symptoms are a complication of panic disorder. This important observation of the typical course of the disorder is reflected in the DSM-III-R classification in which different degrees of phobic avoidance are classified as subtypes of panic disorder. The apparently rare cases of agoraphobia that are seen clinically and that do not develop secondary to panic disorder are diagnosed as agoraphobia without history of panic disorder."[12]

Limited Symptom Attacks

The category labeled agoraphobia without history of panic disorder speaks of a new entity called limited symptom attacks. "DSM-III-R recognizes the concept of a limited symptom attack, i.e. an attack of anxiety that does not meet the symptomatic criteria for a panic attack. This specification distinguishes cases that are associated with sub-panic attacks of anxiety (which may represent mild forms of panic disorder), and cases without attacks. . . . Attacks involving four or more symptoms are arbitrarily defined as panic attacks; attacks involving fewer than four symptoms are limited symptom attacks. . . . It is unclear whether agoraphobia without history of panic disorder with limited symptom attacks represents a variant of panic disorder with agoraphobia. . . ."[12]

The concept of limited symptom attacks adds another nuance to the panic disorder story, and another differential diagnosis to consider when faced with paroxysmal physical symptoms of uncertain etiology. These "masked" or "partial" panic attacks should be considered when somatic symptoms dominate the presentation, even when the affective, cognitive, or behavioral components of a panic attack are absent. Sheehan and Sheehan[14] noted that panic disorder, in its early stages, may show itself only in such minor attacks. "Limited symptom attacks may be a harbinger of progression to the full syndrome . . . as antipanic therapy is effective, both unexpected and situational limited-symptom attacks may be the last vestige of the disorder or continue to represent residual disorder."[15]

Clinical Vignette: Wanda

The following case will illustrate a presentation where a limited or minor symptom attack caused much clinical confusion. Wanda was 28 years old, mildly mentally retarded, with a full scale IQ of 64. She was referred by an ENT colleague with a complaint of dizziness and balance loss. A complete workup, including audiologic assessment, neurological evaluation, CAT scan of the head with contrast, and EEG had all proved to be noncontributory. He now suspected an emotional cause.

Wanda's history showed her first episode of dizziness and unsteadiness to have occurred approximately three years previously. These attacks stopped after eight months, to return 28 months later. I saw her for the first time four months after this recrudescence. As noted, she had been seen by her family physician, an ENT specialist, and a neurologist. My evaluation revealed that she had been having recurrent attacks of anxiety during which she trembled, felt dizzy and unsteady on her feet, and felt frustrated and scared.

She was withdrawn, showing a decrease in her general activity and social interaction. This avoidance behavior, which verged on agoraphobia, was due entirely to her fear that she would have an attack of dizziness if she went out. She was no longer attending the vocational workshop where she had been for two years.

Nor was she attending social functions through a local MR Group, which she had enjoyed. There was also clinical evidence of moderate depression. She had had a ten-pound weight loss. Her history also showed the death of a favorite and attentive grandmother several years before. She responded beautifully to individual psychotherapy and chemotherapy.

The Benefits of Awareness

Controversy aside, as a clinician, I feel that this new awareness of panic disorder has led to our ability to make quicker and more accurate diagnoses, and to offer more appropriate and helpful treatment for this widespread emotional problem. In the past, without the concept, many cases were missed, some misdiagnosed, and many treatment attempts were prolonged.

The study of panic disorder continues to evolve. The last decade has been exciting. We are constantly being alerted to new etiologic and treatment considerations. However, in spite of our new awareness, panic disorder still often remains a hidden emotional problem. Many suffer silently, not understanding their painful and limiting disability. This chapter has offered an historical perspective of the classification of anxiety, including the emergence of the concept of panic disorder as a separate diagnostic entity in 1980, and the more recent—1987—nosological revisions. Let us continue to look at some of its other aspects and gain additional insight, so that perhaps some of these undiagnosed sufferers may be helped and can once again lead full productive lives.

3

Panic Disorder
A Special Anxiety State

Clinical Vignette: Ray

The feeling was overwhelming. Ray could never remember being as frightened. He had been washing up before bed when it happened. Suddenly, out of the blue, his body was engulfed by a feeling of dread and impending doom. The sudden rush of anxiety had a crescendo effect, like waves that would not stop beating against the shore.

He wanted to scream. He wanted to run and get help. He wanted to hide. But he could not focus his mind to cope with the onslaught of terror. His heart raced and seemed to want to jump out of his chest. He was short of breath and felt as if he was smothering.

He tried to walk but was weak and unsteady on his feet. When he finally got to the bed, he lay there huddled and trembling, sure that he was dying or having a heart attack. He would later learn that he had had his first panic attack.

What Is Panic Disorder?

Patients often complain of anxiety and tension. But panic disorder is different. As you can see from the above clinical vignette, anxiety reaches the level of a panic attack when it is overwhelming and associated with personality disorganization, an inability to function, and signs of intense arousal of the autonomic nervous system. A full-blown panic disorder is characterized by panic symptoms or attacks that occur with enough frequency to be disabling or impairing. "Panic disorder is the anxiety disorder that primary care physicians are most likely to encounter in their practices; in its fully developed manifestation, it is also the most serious and disabling of all anxiety disorders."[1]

Definition: DSM-III-R Criteria

According to the *Diagnostic and Statistical Manual of Mental Disorders* (DSM-III-R),[2] published in May 1987, the diagnostic criteria for panic disorder indicate that when these attacks of sudden and intense anxiety occur four times in a four-week period (or one or more attacks have been followed by a period of at least a month of persistent fear of having another attack), the attacks have progressed to a panic disorder. The attacks have to be unexpected and not triggered by situations in which the person was the focus of another's attention.

The person must feel apprehensive or fearful, and at least four symptoms of physiologic or somatic anxiety, and/or some expression of feeling fearful that they will become totally helpless or out of control, must have appeared during at least one of the attacks. During at least some of the attacks, at least four of the physical symptoms must develop suddenly and increase in intensity within 10 minutes of the beginning of the first somatic symptom noticed in the attack. An organic factor cannot be present which initiates and maintains the disturbance.

The following are the symptoms associated with panic disorder:

Palpitations *or false perception of rapid HR*
Shortness of breath *or shallow breathing*
Chest pains (usually in a young person, and nonexertional) *or chest pressure*

Choking or smothering sensations
Dizziness or unsteadiness
Numbness or tingling sensations
Hot or cold flashes
Sweating
Trembling or shaking
Nausea, diarrhea, or abdominal distress
Feeling weak or faint
Depersonalization or derealization
Fear of going crazy, dying, or losing control
Feeling of impending doom

these are the worst

"The panic attacks usually last minutes or, more rarely, hours."[2] "Actual panic attacks are sudden and develop swiftly, lasting 20 to 30 minutes at most . . . the patient who describes panic lasting for many hours or many days either is confusing residual feelings of anxiety with the actual panic attack or suffering from a condition other than panic disorder."[3]

Some people with panic disorder may develop varying degrees of nervousness and apprehension between attacks. When this is focused only on the fear of having another attack, it is called anticipatory anxiety. In that patients are very frightened and fearful of having a panic attack, it is not unusual for a low-grade chronic anticipatory anxiety to develop secondarily as they become watchful for future attacks. Anticipatory anxiety possesses many of the features of generalized anxiety, including constant motor tension, autonomic hyperactivity, apprehension, hypervigilance, and initial insomnia. However, in these cases, the additional diagnosis of generalized anxiety disorder is not made. Some people with a panic disorder may also show chronic generalized anxiety between panic attacks.

Who Gets Panic Disorder?

Ray is not alone. Anxiety problems, expressed directly as a subjective emotion associated with a variety of physical symptoms, such as seen in generalized anxiety, panic disorder, and posttraumatic stress disorder, or controlled unconsciously by the production of phobias, obsessive-compulsive, or dissociative symptoms, affect 7–15 percent of adults. Anxiety was confirmed as being the most common mental illness by the National Institute of Mental Health multisite Epidemiologic Catchment Area (ECA) program, which was conducted between 1980 and 1983 at five sites in the United States.[4]

The ECA survey found a six-month incidence of panic disorder in nearly 1 percent of the population and a lifetime incidence of 1.5 percent. The survey also found that 9 percent of adults experience fear or panic symptoms. Because of changing diagnostic criteria and various "masked" forms of panic, its 1 percent six-month prevalence may be an underestimate. Weissman and Merikangas reviewed the results of four epidemiological studies of anxiety disorders. They reported prevalence rates (one month to one year) for panic disorder ranging from 0.4 to 1.2 per 100 persons.[5] Others have stated that panic disorder affects about 5 percent of the population.[6] Of patients seen by cardiologists, 10 to 14 percent are afflicted with panic disorder.[7]

Panic disorder is the disease of poets Percy Bysshe Shelley and Emily Dickinson. It is more common in women than in men. Prevalence rates are higher in the separated and divorced. It usually begins during late adolescence or early adult life, a time of choices, transition, separation, and added responsibility. The mean age of onset in one study was 26.3 years.[8] Panic disorder patients often show a family history of anxiety disorders. First-degree relatives of patients with panic disorder are at a markedly higher risk of developing the disorder.[8] Over the course of the illness, patients are at greater risk for death from unnatural causes, especially suicide.[9]

The Panic-Prone Person

The personality characteristics of those who develop panic disorder vary considerably. However, in the author's clinical experience, they often have certain factors in common. Cross-sectional studies of patients with panic disorder or agoraphobia have demonstrated personality traits of dependency, avoidance, low self-esteem, and interpersonal sensitivity.[10]

There is no prototypical Minnesota Multiphasic Personality Inventory (MMPI) profile in these patients. The majority of patients with panic disorder appear well functioning on the MMPI, although somewhat anxious and introverted. About 25 percent display significant personality pathology marked by dependency, interpersonal hypersensitivity, somatization, hopelessness, and self-blame.[11]

The common attributes or premorbid personality of the panic-prone person is often a picture of contradictions and a battle between conflicting needs. These individuals greatly value control. Any loss or threatened loss of control causes them to feel anxious. Changes in their life that upset their balance often make them feel as if they will lose control, a very frightening feeling for them. The problem, however, is often not so much loss of control as a need for too much control to begin with.

Panic-prone persons overvalue their independence and feel great discomfort in acknowledging their dependency needs. For this reason, they are often reluctant to accept help. They prefer to help others. They are usually not aware that they need people but have difficulty separating from those close to them. They may show particular signs of distress at times of change and loss due to divorce or geographical relocation. They tend to repress their feelings and feel anxious when their emotions surface. They feel more comfortable intellectualizing and rationalizing. They tend to be perfectionist, compulsive individuals, with high expectations of themselves and others.

Lastly, panic-prone people are avoidant people. They are prone to passive-avoidance behavior, and often channel their feelings into activity or concentrating on others. It is often difficult to pin them down to specifics. In conversation, even in therapy, they will focus on anything but that which is really bothering them. For this reason, they may have to be questioned carefully to obtain information about their symptoms if you suspect a diagnosis of panic disorder.

Typical Course or Presentation

After 1980, psychiatrists started to gain some insight into this new anxiety state. A typical course or presentation began to emerge. Young adults in their twenties, more commonly female, with perhaps a history of separation anxiety and a family member with a history of anxiety, panic, or phobic disorders, start to develop sudden attacks of anxiety following or during a period of great stress. During these attacks, they experience chest pain and/or some other physical symptoms. Scared and fearful, restless and jumpy, they run to the hospital emergency room or to their family physician.

Usually, the primary physician will offer reassurance and do a sufficient medical workup to rule out a physical cause for the specific complaint. Others may try to rule out other physical conditions that can cause similar symptoms or show anxiety as a symptom. Hypoglycemia, hyperthyroidism, caffeine or amphetamine intoxication, drug withdrawal, asthma, premenstrual syndrome/menopausal syndrome, temporal lobe epilepsy, or even Addison's disease may be considered.

No physical disease is found. However, the patient, in disbelief, continues to worry that some dread disease must be lurking in the background and causing these changes. Either by self or physician referral, the patient may start a long quest involving multiple consultative visits with various specialists and more sophisticated diagnostic tests. It may be some time before the diagnosis of panic disorder is made and/or the patient accepts an emotional cause. Anxious people often rush in many directions to seek an explanation for their feelings. They often look for anything to get rid of their anguish, including fads and magic cures.

Ray followed a similar clinical course. After his first panic attack, he forgot about the incident. Ten days later a second attack occurred. It took the same form as the first. This time he went to the emergency room where he was reassured that no medical problem existed.

During the next year, he continued to have episodic attacks of overwhelming anxiety. Fearful that he was having a heart attack, he made multiple trips back to the emergency room. During these times, he tended to focus on the chest discomfort that stood out in his mind as the primary symptom. His father had died of a heart attack several years before. During his "attacks," Ray sensed impending doom and felt that he also would die.

His hopeless and helpless demeanor during these times were in direct contrast to his usual independent and productive personality. He was 30 years old. At work, he was known as a bright, conscientious achiever who had excellent potential to climb the corporate ladder. After a long period of stressful anticipation, he had finally, recently, been given a promotion with a considerable increase in responsibility. He wished his father was here to see his success. They had not been close, but Ray had relied on him for emotional support during problem-fraught times.

Repeated cardiac evaluations, including a stress test and 24-hour cardiac monitoring, and an echocardiagram, showed mitral valve prolapse but no symptoms of cardiac disease. This was very frustrating. There must be some physical explanation for his unbearable pain. His family physician and a cardiologist all confirmed the emergency room physician's opinion and suggested an emotional basis for his attacks. His girlfriend was also frustrated with him and suggested that he grow up. He continued to be upset an [1] convinced that he had heart disease.

Other Clinical Presentations

Although the above is a very typical way that panic disorder may present, a variety of clinical complaints may signal the presence of this syndrome. "Some patients present in a straightforward way with panic episodes as their primary and only complaint. Others present with symptoms related to panic disorder, such as phobic avoidance or anticipatory anxiety. Still others present with other psychiatric or medical problems in which panic may not be immediately apparent."[12] As we shall see in the next chapter, panic disorder is also often difficult to diagnose due to the fact that it may mimic a physical disorder and/or show different confusing physical symptoms. Because of its association with heart, respiratory, and gastrointestinal symptoms, "probably more cardiologists and gastroenterologists see people with panic disorder than psychiatrists."[6]

Shear and Frances,[12] in a 1988 article on the clinical presentation of panic disorder, list the following psychiatric and medical symptoms that may serve as presenting complaints in patients who meet the criteria for panic disorder. It is important to question these patients about the presence of panic symptoms.

Psychiatric Symptoms as Presenting Complaints
     Depression
     Substance Abuse
     Phobias
     Depersonalization
     Hypochondriasis
     Sleep Disturbance
     Eating Disturbances
     Marital Problems

Physical Symptoms as Presenting Complaints
     Breathing Problems
     Chest Pain
     Dizziness
     Gastrointestinal distress

Headaches ✓
Blurred vision

An Irritable Bowel Syndrome Presentation

no kidding!

"Functional bowel disease comprises a group of disorders with chronic or recurrent gastrointestinal symptoms that are not explained by structural abnormalities, infection, or metabolic changes."[13] Irritable bowel syndrome is probably the most common digestive disorder seen in medical practice, possibly affecting some 22 million Americans.[14] "Epidemiologic studies indicate that, in Western societies, up to one-third of adults report functional gastrointestinal symptoms. Perhaps 14 to 22 percent of them are described as consistent with IBS."[13]

IBS is also related to migraine!

The symptoms of irritable bowel syndrome can be triggered by anxiety, tension, and emotional stress. Like panic disorder, it usually appears in late adolescence or early adulthood and appears in women more often than in men. In a recent issue of *Postgraduate Medicine*,[15] Marshall appropriately poses the question, "Are some irritable bowel syndromes actually panic disorder?" in his article by that title. This is a new area of interest in the area of diagnosis of panic disorder.

A 1986 report[16] described five patients with panic disorder and irritable bowel syndrome. Both the panic and gastrointestinal symptoms abated dramatically and rapidly after pharmacologic treatment of the panic symptoms in all five patients. The authors speculated that the gastrointestinal symptoms may have been symptoms of panic disorder, rather than a separate condition aggravated by the anxiety disorder. Other au-

thors have also noted the wide range of nongastroin-
testinal symptoms found in irritable bowel syndrome.
Of these patients, 70–90 percent are said to have diag-
nosable psychiatric problems, especially anxiety and depression.[17,18] Marshall feels that if there is a subset of
IBS patients whose symptoms are manifestations of an
underlying panic disorder, they will be of the diarrheal
or loose-stool type (particularly if the patient describes
an acute sense of urgency), will respond to antipanic
drugs, and will show the criteria for diagnosis of panic
disorder upon careful questioning.[15]

Clinical Vignette: Andrew

The following is an example of such a gastrointestinal presentation. Andrew's daily morning experience of abdominal cramping and diarrhea was
becoming more frequent. He had always shown stress
through his G.I. tract, but these attacks were something
different. They were also starting to happen at other
times of the day. During these times, he had an urgent
need to move his bowels, felt extremely anxious, became weak, unsteady on his feet, and thought that he
would faint. He sensed impending doom and felt that
he would die.

These bouts of anxiety were in direct contrast to
Andrew's outward persona of organized efficiency. He
had tremendous drive to succeed. At 26, he was already
being considered for a vice presidency in the corporation. He had been living in his own apartment for three
years since graduating with his MBA. He was sometimes lonely but had been relieved to leave his parental
home. His father, successful, but controlling and tense,

was prone to episodes of chest pain, hyperventilation, and shortness of breath which seemed to have no physical cause. His mother drank.

Andrew had seen his family physician, been referred for a upper and lower G.I., been probed and proctosigmoidoscoped, and had a battery of blood tests. All had been normal. It was suggested that he had an "irritable colon." He felt that the doctor was not telling him the truth. There must be something wrong with his body if this was happening. He visited a specialist for a second opinion.

The answer was the same. Andrew continued to worry and to feel that he had some hidden dread disease. Several months later, he was referred for psychiatric consultation and a diagnosis of panic disorder was made. Both his emotional and physical symptoms responded to antipanic medication.

Relationship to Substance Abuse

Substance abuse and panic disorder show various relationships. Substance abuse can be a complication of panic disorder. Patients may self-medicate themselves to relieve their feelings of anxiety. They can thus become psychologically and physiologically dependent on drugs, such as alcohol, sleeping pills, and minor tranquilizers. Panic attacks can also be seen during drug (barbiturates, antidepressant, or tranquilizers) and alcohol withdrawal. Here it is often difficult to tell which is primary, unless a thorough history is taken. Panic attacks can also be seen in caffeine or amphetamine intoxication.

"Alcoholism is often found in the families of people with panic disorder. Since alcoholics commonly have anxiety attacks, particularly when hung over, it is hard to tell which came first—panic disorder or alcoholism. Both typically begin in the teens and twenties."[6] Richard S. Hallam[19] has made the point that "it is possible that panic anxiety and alcohol dependence have common antecedents and overlapping features." He gives two possible reasons for this association. "The first is that the use of alcohol is simply a means of reducing anxiety complaints. The second is that agoraphobia and alcohol dependence are sex-related expressions of some common antecedent conditions." Studies have shown that females stay at home as a coping mechanism, whereas males use alcohol, which is more consistent with expectations for males, to deal with similar issues.

Drug use can also produce panic attacks. People who use marijuana or cannabis may suffer from short-lived, acute anxiety states, which may reach such proportions as to be called panic attacks. Such panic attacks probably constitute the most frequent adverse reaction to the moderate smoking of marijuana. Adverse psychological effects are also common with amphetamine use. Anxiety and fear to the point of acute panic have been reported. Cocaine can also cause undesirable symptoms including high blood pressure, racing heart, anxiety, and paranoia. The most common adverse effect of LSD and related drugs is the "bad trip," which resembles the acute panic reaction to cannabis, but can be more severe.

Possible Resolutions of Panic Disorder

Just as panic disorder may present in multiple ways, without treatment, it may also show various patterns of resolution. Some cases will show a spontaneous

cessation of symptoms and/or go into remission for
many years, only to appear again during a period of
extreme stress. Some patients, although no longer having actual panic attacks, will be plagued by anticipatory
anxiety for some time. Others will be left with limited
symptoms or "minor" attacks. Many will become agoraphobic and housebound, or develop other secondary
avoidance behaviors. Here, they may become so inca-
pacitated and dysfunctional that they will to all intents
and purposes forget about their initial panic attacks. In
desperation, hoping to block the panic attacks, some
may self-medicate with alcohol or drugs and create additional problems. Still others will progress to a hypo-
chondriacal or somatic resolution.

In a somatization disorder outcome, the patient
may selectively and chronically focus on one specific
frightening physical symptom or body area (e.g., cardiac complaints). Gradually, they may minimize, deny,
or simply stop mentioning their other anxiety symptoms, and use this one complaint to completely explain
their secondary avoidance behavior. Here again, unless
a thorough history is taken, the physician may focus on
the one or two somatic complaints presented and miss
the original primary diagnosis of panic disorder. This
can prolong misdiagnosis for some time.

Common presentations include cardiac, neurological, and gastrointestinal symptoms. Katon, in a
retrospective study of 55 patients, showed that panic
disorder is an important cause of somatization in primary care. He wisely notes that "viewing patients as
having either a medical or psychiatric illness may ob-
scure an important diagnosis that is exacerbating the
patient's problem."[20] The clinical picture is further complicated as the patient gets older and may actually develop a real physical problem in one of these areas.

Such a dilemma was presented by the elderly patient, Rose.

Clinical Vignette: Rose

This 76-year-old woman was a constant source of frustration to the nursing staff. She had been hospitalized psychiatrically for depression and agitation some days previously. Her almost nightly cry of chest pain and loud bell ringing to signal for help had become almost a ritual. There was a documented history of cardiac disease. However, repeated cardiograms and physical evaluation by the internal medicine department showed no acute pathology. Although she admitted reluctantly that she was anxious, it took many talks and pointed questioning to establish that she was actually having panic attacks, with a primary symptom of chest discomfort.

History finally revealed that she had been having these attacks for 40 years. During the preponderance of this time, she had focused on her cardiac symptoms and had undergone multiple workups. The situation was further complicated when she actually did develop angina ten years ago.

Relationship to Pregnancy

An interesting recent finding is the relationship between panic symptoms and pregnancy. George et al.[21] published the report of three women with panic disorder who showed marked improvement in their panic symptoms during pregnancy. The improvement was not attributable to medication, psychotherapy, or stabilization of life situations. After delivery, the attacks returned in their previous intensity. The attacks decreased again in subsequent pregnancies.

Three explanations are offered for this possible antipanic effect of pregnancy. Pregnancy may stabilize and blunt the sympathoadrenal response to some simple physiologic stimuli and thus oppose the greater lability of noradrenergic control of the sympathetic nervous system that has been suggested in panic disorder, and prevent the paroxysmal activity of sympathetic function seen during a panic attack. It is next suggested that the hormonal changes in pregnancy may exert an anxiolytic effect by means of interactions with barbiturate receptors. Lastly, we are reminded that the positive emotional effects of pregnancy, such as the sense of purpose and self-esteem that planned pregnancy may bring could be responsible for improving psychological function. Continued verification of this effect of pregnancy on panic attacks could have clinical management and etiological implications.

The Emotional Problem of the 1980s

As we begin to understand panic disorder better, we are becoming aware of the multitudes of people who are affected. In spite of more recent media reporting of this disorder, panic disorder remains a hidden emotional problem. Many laymen and some health professionals are still unaware of its vicissitudes or the very real potential for its successful treatment. Although a very significant psychological problem, seen frequently in clinical practice, very little has been written on this subject in either the popular or psychiatric press. Many undiagnosed victims suffer silently, not understanding their painful and limiting disability. The DSM-III-R comments under the topic of prevalence that "the disorder is common"[2]—certainly an understatement. In all probability, panic disorder is veritably the emotional problem of the 1980s.

As we have seen, panic disorder is a complex malady with frightening symptoms. It is difficult to diagnose due to its confusing physical and emotional interplay. Overall, the diagnosis of panic disorder requires an evaluation of the total symptom complex and the identification of a *pattern*, rather than of individual *components*. Once it is understood, it can be treated and eradicated. The first step in this process is medical education. A greater awareness and understanding of this widespread emotional problem needs to be gained. Physicians, psychiatrists, and mental health professionals need to recognize its symptoms, clinical interrelationships, and associated complications. This will allow you to look at your patients' complaints in a new way, producing more efficient diagnoses and treatment plans.

4

The Great Pretender
Differential Diagnosis of Panic Disorder

O lift me from the grass!
I die! I faint! I fail!
My cheek is cold & white, alas!
My heart beats loud and fast.
                    Percy Bysshe Shelley
                    Indian Serenade

"The sounds of emotional distress are unique. Patients communicate anxiety and tension either directly or couched in other emotional or physical symptoms and complaints. If the diagnosis is panic disorder, the words will be different. We will have to listen even more carefully to hear the cry of emotional pain and stress."[1]

Because of the physical focus that accompanies panic disorder, people often seek medical attention during and after attacks. Differential diagnosis can be confusing. This was true even in Elizabethan times when the hero of Shelley's poem might have been seen as having the "vapors," being lovesick, or having some physical malady. Many generations later the physician will still have to rule out many emotional problems and physical disorders in a variety of body systems when dealing with the symptoms of panic disorder. "The diagnosis is made only when it cannot be established that an organic factor initiated and maintained the disturbance."[2]

Patients with panic disorder present with symptoms suggestive of multiple system involvement. A good medical workup must be sufficient to rule out various etiological possibilities for the specific physical chief complaint(s). One must also think of other organic conditions that can cause similar symptoms or show anxiety as a symptom.

A significant number of patients who visit cardiovascular, gastrointestinal, and neurologic clinics meet the criteria for a diagnosis of panic disorder.[3] Other psychiatric disorders that may resemble panic must also be considered. As you can see, panic disorder often presents a difficult differential diagnosis. Because of its diagnostic complexities and its tendency to mimic many physical and psychological syndromes, I refer to panic disorder as The Great Pretender.

Another issue here that has gained recent research interest, is the idea of co-morbity. Co-morbidity refers to the increased probability of one disorder's being present given the presence of another. The co-morbidity data gathered during the ECA survey demonstrates the need for clinicians to search carefully for the presence of coexisting disorders when treating patients with anxiety disorders. For instance, coexisting disorders found with panic disorder include depression, alcohol abuse, and agoraphobia.

The following is a list of the mental and physical possibilities that need to be excluded in the differential diagnosis of panic disorder:

Psychiatric Disorders to Consider in the Differential Diagnosis of Panic Attacks/Disorder
1. Depression
2. Other anxiety disorders
3. Schizophrenia
4. Organic brain syndrome
5. Somatoform disorder/Hypochondria
6. Sleep disturbance

Physical Conditions That Can Mimic Panic Symptoms or Present with Panic-like Episodes
A. Cardiovascular
   1. Arrhythmias
   2. Angina

    3. Hyperkinetic heart syndrome
    4. Mitral valve prolapse
  B. Respiratory
    1. Asthma
    2. Acute exacerbation of chronic lung disease
    3. Pulmonary emboli (recurrent)
    4. Hyperventilation syndrome
  C. Endocrine
    1. Hyperthyroidism
    2. Hypothyroidism
    3. Hypoglycemia
    4. Hyperparathyroidism
    5. Hypoparathyroidism
    6. Cushing's syndrome
    7. Addison's disease
    8. Pheochromocytoma
    9. Premenstrual syndrome/Menopausal syndrome
  D. Drug-Related
    1. Intoxication (stimulant abuse)
      a. amphetamine
      b. cocaine
      c. appetite suppressants
      d. caffeine
    2. Withdrawal
      a. alcohol
      b. narcotics
      c. sedative hypnotics
  E. Neurologic
    1. Temporal lobe epilepsy (partial, complex seizures)
    2. Vertigo (Ménière's disease, acute labyrinthitis)

Differentiation from Other Psychiatric Disorders

Depression

Symptoms of depression and anxiety disorders may overlap. They can share in common a dysphoric mood, sleep disturbances, weight disturbances, indecisiveness, agitation, and somatic complaints. "During a major depressive episode there may be recurrent unexpected panic attacks, in which case diagnoses of both a mood disorder and panic disorder should be made."[2] The data on co-morbidity indicate that in a patient with a major depression, the risk of panic disorder is increased by a factor of 18.8.[4]

"The distinction between panic disorder and depression has generated a great deal of scientific controversy and clinical confusion."[5] Because panic attacks respond to treatment with tricyclic antidepressants and monoamine oxidase inhibitors, but do not respond to most antianxiety agents, some investigators have speculated that panic disorder may be a form of depression. However, although it is probably true that patients with panic disorder are at greater risk of developing depression than are normals, at this time there is no reason to believe that panic disorder is another form of affective disorder.[6] (Refer to "Classification Controversies" in Chapter 2.)

Other Anxiety Disorders

Anxiety is the prominent feature of all the anxiety disorders, including agoraphobia, social and simple phobia, obsessive-compulsive disorder, posttraumatic stress disorder, and generalized anxiety disorder. All need to be differentiated from panic disorder.

Although generalized anxiety disorder (GAD) and panic disorder may share the symptoms of motor tension, autonomic hyperactivity, and vigilance and scanning seen with panic attacks, duration in GAD is longer and does not feature the autonomic arousal, somatic characteristics of panic disorder. Those suffering from GAD do not report the sudden spikes of anxiety level seen in panic. Those who suffer from GAD and panic will be able to describe the difference in clinical presentation. They will see their panic attacks as a unique event involving a sudden massive increase in anxiety level, which then quickly subsides. The GAD patient will talk of a more gradual onset and a less severe intensity.

In patients who have suffered anticipatory anxiety in conjunction with their panic attacks for a long time, it may be difficult to distinguish this from GAD unless the patient is questioned carefully. The focus of concern in anticipatory anxiety is only on the fear of having another panic attack and not on other worries or issues. (Refer to Chapter 2 for additional information on the diagnostic criteria for generalized anxiety disorder.)

At times, overwhelming traumatic events occur that have the potential to hit the very core of the individual and leave them feeling totally helpless, enraged, and unable to cope with everyday life. These events can produce a specific cluster of psychological and physical symptoms called a posttraumatic stress disorder. The DSM-III, published in 1980, that brought panic disorder into our nomenclature, also gave this old clinical problem a fresh veneer, including a new name and expanded clinical criteria. Like its cousin, panic disorder, it also shows symptoms of hyperarousal. However, this syndrome is clearly related to "an event outside of the range of usual human experience that would be markedly distressing to almost anyone."[2] It also features recollections, dreams, and flashbacks of the traumatic event as well as avoidance criteria of diminished responsiveness in reference to the trauma and the world in general.

As you have seen, panic disorder patients can develop avoidance behavior such as phobias, particularly agoraphobia. This term, derived from the Greek "agora," the large open marketplace next to the Acropolis in ancient Athens, means "fear of the marketplace." It refers to the "fear of being in places or situations from which escape might be difficult (or embarrassing) or in which help might not be available in the event of suddenly developing a symptom(s) that could be incapacitating or extremely embarrassing."[2]

The DSM-III-R also includes a category of agoraphobia without history of panic disorder. "In panic disorder with agoraphobia, the panic attacks may be in full remission while the agoraphobia persists, but a history of panic disorder would preclude a current diagnosis of agoraphobia without history of panic disorder."[2] The co-morbidity odds ratio of agoraphobics developing panic disorder is 18.0.[4]

The remaining categories of phobia, simple phobia and social phobia, usually are not associated with spontaneous panic attacks. The essential feature of social phobia is "a persistent fear of one or more situations in which the person is exposed to possible scrutiny by others and fears that he or she may do something or act in a way that will be humiliating or embarrassing."[2] The essential feature of a simple phobia is "a persistent fear of a circumscribed stimulus other than fear of having a panic attack or of humiliation or embarrassment in certain social situations."[2]

These can include fear of animals, bodily injury, closed spaces, heights, or air travel. These phobias have an earlier age of onset than panic disorder and/or agoraphobia.[7] Unlike panic disorder, these two phobias have a questionable response to pharmacologic treatment[8,9] and are more appropriately treated with behavioral therapy.

Obsessive-compulsive disorders involve 0.5 percent of the population. They are characterized by recurrent thoughts or actions that are accompanied by a sense of subjective compulsion and a desire to resist it. Obsessions are persistent ideas, thoughts, impulses, or images that are experienced as intrusive and senseless (e.g., repetitive thoughts of violence, contamination, or doubt).

Compulsions are repetitive, purposeful, and intentional behaviors that are performed in response to an obsession, according to certain rules, or in a stereotyped fashion (e.g., hand-washing, counting, checking, and touching). When the person attempts to resist a compulsion, there is a sense of mounting tension and anxiety that can be frightening and overwhelming. Carrying out the activity provides a release of tension.

Psychoses

Panic disorder patients often feel that they are going crazy or will "lose their minds." "However, Klein has evidence that the incidence of psychotic illness in panic patients is no higher than the incidence of *schizophrenia* in the general population."[5] As we shall see, reassurance that their panic attacks do not mean that they are psychotic is often one of the first steps in the successful treatment of the disorder. "In severe cases, their reduced level of functioning may resemble that of a schizophrenic disorder with associated anxiety. However, the withdrawal and constriction of activities, the psychotic component, poor premorbid history, and family history characteristic of schizophrenia should make this differentiation clear."[10]

I have seen incidences when manic-depressive patients suffer bouts of intense anxiety following a period of psychotic regression. This often starts to happen as they return to their normal routine, particularly following a period of hospitalization. These episodes of anxiety can resemble panic attacks, but usually seem to resolve after a few weeks.

Organic Brain Syndrome

Organic anxiety syndrome can show recurrent panic attacks. However, a specific organic factor can always be demonstrated that is etiologically related to the disturbance.

Somatoform Disorders/Hypochondriasis

Panic patients and somatoform patients both have multiple medical complaints and numerous physician visits and consultations. Both are anxious about their health and convinced that they have an underlying medical illness. Differentiation here hinges on the presence of identifiable panic attacks. Some feel that somatoform patients are more difficult to convince that nothing is medically wrong after a thorough medical workup and will continue to complain of a variety of aches and pains.[5]

Sleep Disturbance

Panic patients at times complain of attacks that wake them during the night or occur as they are falling asleep. "Patients with a chief complaint of insomnia may be suffering from sleep-related panic. Careful questioning reveals the sleep disturbance is caused by panic episodes, which occur at sleep onset or during the sleep cycle."[11] A large percentage of panic episodes occur in relation to sleep.[12] These nocturnal panic attacks occur during slow wave, not REM sleep[13] and may be related to the phenomenon of relaxation-induced panic.

Differentiation from Medical Conditions

Cardiovascular System

"The relationship between the human psyche and the cardiovascular system has been appreciated for centuries, since Celsus in 30 A.D. noted that many experiences of everyday life affect the pulse."[14] Recent studies reveal that a high percentage of patients with chest pain and normal coronary arteries meet the criteria for panic disorder.[15] Although cardiovascular symptoms (palpitations, tachycardia, chest pain) are common with panic attacks, no significant cardiac pathology has been associated with the disorder. Arrhythmias (especially tachyarrhythmias), episodes of anginal chest pain, hyperdynamic, and beta-adrenergic circulatory state all may be confused with panic attacks.

Panic disorder is statistically more common in patients with mitral valve prolapse.[3] The prevalence ranges from 0 to 50 percent.[16] Although there are many unresolved issues with regard to the relationship between the two disorders, there is no evidence to date that mitral valve prolapse causes panic disorder. There is also no pathophysiologic or genetic linkage between these disorders.[17] Mitral valve prolapse is generally a benign condition, with an uneventful course, that requires little or no treatment in the majority of patients. Once its presence is established, the physician should reassure the patient. Panic responds no differently to pharmacological treatment at provocation whether mitral valve prolapse is present or not.

Respiratory System

Breathing problems, such as air hunger and shortness of breath, are often a prominent feature of panic attacks. Various causes of hypoxia, including anemias, asthma, and exacerbations of chronic lung disease, may lead to symptoms of anxiety and must be ruled out.

Hyperventilation syndrome, like panic disorder, can also produce a variety of psychological and physical symptoms. John R. Marshall, in a 1987 article, commented on the relationship between the two syndromes. He concludes that "criteria that permit a clear discrimination between these disorders have not been developed . . . hyperventilation syndrome should be abandoned as a separate diagnosis or distinct disorder . . . the majority of the phenomena now called hyperventilation syndrome is . . . a subset of symptoms occurring secondarily to the central dysregulation now known in psychiatry as panic disorder."[18]

Endocrine System

"The widespread effects of hormones on various target organs and neurotransmitters can lead to a plethora of symptoms that are similar to those of anxiety attacks. Abnormalities of thyroid, parathyroid, adrenal, and pancreatic hormone function have been reported to present with symptoms of anxiety . . . Appropriate screening tests should be used to rule them out."[10]

Pheochromocytoma, a catecholamine-producing tumor, although rare, may mimic panic attacks with symptoms of tremor, palpitations, flushing, and sweating. It may also show headache and elevated blood pressure. However, the paroxysmal attacks here "are not as frequent or as intense as in primary anxiety disorder. The somatic components dominate over the cognitive [emotional] symptoms, and phobic avoidance behavior is not found."[19]

Thyroid disease is known to be frequently associated with psychological symptoms. Hyperthyroidism, hypothyroidism and, less commonly, hyperparathyroidism can masquerade as panic attacks. Various authors have reviewed case reports that suggest that thyroid disease may have a specific relationship to panic disorder, in some patients preceding the development of panic disorder.[19,20] Panic attacks often persist even after the thyroid abnormality is corrected. Although many patients give a history of thyroid disease, laboratory tests do not confirm the relationship. Longitudinal studies will be needed to enhance our understanding here.

Reactive or idiopathic hypoglycemia is often listed as a condition that can produce symptoms similar to panic attacks. It is true that a diabetic who suffers a sudden drop in serum glucose level after excess insulin has been injected will show signs of diffuse diaphoresis, tachycardia, lethargy, tremulousness, light-headedness, and anxiety, in addition to hunger. However, it is unlikely that this extreme hypoglycemia would occur in the nondiabetic, medically healthy person, or that hypoglycemia is a routine cause of panic attacks.

Drug-Related Conditions

A careful medication and substance use/abuse history should be taken in all patients suspected of having panic attacks. The substance abuse may be the primary diagnosis. Stimulant drug intoxications (caffeine or amphetamines) may show panic attacks. Acute central nervous system depressant drug (barbiturates, antidepressants, or tranquilizers) or alcohol withdrawal may show symptoms that simulate panic attacks, although not typically in the form of brief, episodic attacks. In reference to co-morbidity, a patient with panic disorder is 4.3 times as likely as the general population to have an alcohol abuse disorder.[4]

Neurologic Disorders

"Episodic bursts of vertigo sometimes accompanied by light-headedness, nausea, vomiting, and anxiety, can be caused by a number of medical conditions. These include lesions of the cerebellum, brain stem, or eighth cranial nerve, acute labyrinthitis, benign postional vertigo, and Ménière's disease. Although this symptom complex is difficult to differentiate from a panic attack, such medical patients often complain of true vertigo, not dizziness or light-headedness. They feel that the room or their body is spinning in the same direction with each attack. Consultation with an otolaryngologist or neurologist is necessary if such conditions are suspected."[5]

Temporal lobe epilepsy or partial complex seizures are a fascinating disorder that share many features in common with panic disorder. Both occur suddenly without a precipitating event, have a paroxysmal onset, a short duration, and may be accompanied by intense feelings of fear, terror, and unreality. Both show a multitude of somato-sensory autonomic symptoms, such as sweating, flushing, hyperventilation, and tachycardia.

The work of Roth and Harper[20] suggests that the distinguishing features seen in the temporal lobe epilepsy group are episodes of sysphasia, motor automatisms, and progression of attacks to unconsciousness. Partial complex seizures, usually having a temporal lobe origin, seem to have the likeliest resemblance to panic attacks. They "are differentiated by the occurrence of semipurposeful motor or psychic behavior, altered states of consciousness, hallucinations, and progression into other seizure types."[19]

The Panic Disorder Medical Workup

As you can see, the differential diagnosis of panic disorder is complex and multifactorial. Accurate diagnosis is not simple. Panic disorder may present in many ways. Many physical and emotional disorders must be ruled out. It is easy to understand the importance of the physical exam as the first line of defense and an aid in diagnosis. However, the primary physician must also know enough about the emotional aspects of this disorder and his patient's history to be able adequately to evaluate the situation. I offer the following suggested workup and strategies to help you in this evaluation.

History

In the patient whose presenting symptoms seem to meet DSM-III-R criteria for panic disorder, a thorough *history* is important. This should include a family history, to look for evidence of anxiety disorders, affective disorders, and/or alcoholism. A substance use and abuse history must be taken to rule out possible drug intoxication or withdrawal as a possible causative factor. Past medical history, including a systemic review, may show evidence of cardiac, endocrine, gastrointestinal, or neurological disorders.

Physical Examination

A general physical exam should be done, taking a systemic approach. Particularly, look for an enlarged thyroid, hypertension, or cardiac arrhythmias.

Laboratory Screen

A baseline general laboratory screening regimen, including a CBC, serum electrolytes, calcium and phosphorus, thyroid profile (T3, T4, TSH), FBS, renal and hepatic studies, urinalysis, and electrocardiogram should help to diagnose or rule out most of the conditions discussed above under differential diagnosis, or identify those organic disorders that are of clinical significance.

Special Tests

If the physician is alerted by certain signs and symptoms that stand out in the patient's history, physical exam, or abnormal laboratory or ECG, then special or more sophisticated tests can be ordered. For instance, if routine screening shows a reduction in serum calcium, an increase in phosphorus, and a normal alkaline phosphatase, then parathormone levels can be ordered.

Most clinicians now feel that hypoglycemia should seldom cause diagnostic confusion. However, if panic attacks are consistently postprandial, associated with accompanying hunger, or gastric surgery, you may wish to do a glucose tolerance test and insulin assay. Even in such cases, only a three-hour GTT is recommended, since many normal individuals may have hypoglycemia after five- or seven-hour GTTs and this occurrence is of dubious clinical significance.[21]

Routine testing for pheochromocytomas in panic disorder patients is not necessary or recommended. However, if the clinical picture shows headaches, sweating, or marked paroxysmal hypertension, a 24-hour urine for catecholamines (metanephrine and vanillylmandelic acid) would seem appropriate.

Temporal lobe epilepsy is not a consideration in every possible panic disorder patient. Therefore, an EEG does not have to be routine. However, if the patient's history and physical exam suggest an actual neurological deficit with evidence of episodes of dysphasia, motor automatisms, progression of attacks to unconsciousness, or a prominent aura, then a sleep-deprived EEG and a CAT scan of the head are indicated to rule out intracranial pathology.

Stein suggests a general rule that any patient who follows an atypical course or is resistant to standard therapies should be reviewed with a more intensive search for organicity, even in the absence of suspicious symptomatology.[22]

Panic disorder, the great pretender, is a disorder that will keep the clinician on his toes diagnostically. It may present in many ways. Its symptoms may be part of many organic and emotional syndromes. Differential diagnosis requires a detective approach in which the clinician sorts out different clues and evidence, finally being able to say, "I found the culprit, it's called panic disorder."

This chapter has attempted to raise your awareness of the differential diagnosis of this significant emotional problem, help you listen more carefully to how your patients communicate their emotional pain, and be more successful in dealing with panic disorder. Now that we are better able to diagnose this condition, let us look at its various etiological possibilities. For your patient will be asking, "Is my problem emotional or physical?"

5

Panic Disorder
Is It Emotional or Physical?

Pan, in mythology, was the son of Hermes. He was part animal and part human. He was a rural deity; all wild places were his home. He was a noisy, merry god, who was fond of mischief. Like other gods who dwelt in the forest, Pan was dreaded by those whose work forced them to pass through the woods at night. Eerie noises and frightening shadows were common. The gloom and loneliness of this scene often created superstitious fears in the minds of travelers. Thus, sounds heard in the wilderness at night by trembling travelers were attributed to Pan. From this origin, sudden fright without any visible cause was ascribed to Pan, came to bear his name, and was called a "panic" to denote terror or fear. Many years later, the words "panic disorder" still conjure up the overwhelming emotional and physical response of an individual responding to the unknown as he or she passes through the forest of life.

Most panic disorder patients are concerned about the etiology of their illness and want to know if it has a physical or an emotional cause. The etiology of panic disorder remains confusing and conflictual. Some espouse a physical or biological basis. Others feel that the cause is emotional or psychological. The study of panic disorder has become one of the fastest growing areas of research in psychiatry and neurobiology. Given our current knowledge of panic disorder, we are able to provide a patient with the following information about the biological and emotional basis of panic disorder.

Biological (Physical) Theories

The biological theories involve an hypothesis of physical vulnerability or actual defect to explain the cause of panic disorder. Some of these theories include the:

1. Sodium lactate infusion hypothesis
2. Defective biochemical trigger theory (a metabolic instability affecting the locus ceruleus)
3. Hypocalcemia theory (depression of ionized calcium)
4. Hyperventilation theory (respiratory alkalosis)
5. Thermostat theory (regulating the production of natural antianxiety substances which bind to receptors to alleviate anxiety)
6. Focal brain abnormality theory (as demonstrated by PET [positron emission tomography] scan)

Sodium Lactate Infusion Hypothesis

Pitts and McClure[1] were the first to precipitate acute anxiety by lactate infusion. They found that sodium lactate, when given intravenously to normal people, produced some minor discomfort in the form of tremors and paresthesias. However, when given to patients who had an anxiety neurosis, sodium lactate precipitated acute anxiety. This observation led to use of this technique in the laboratory to investigate the physiological and biochemical responses during panic attacks, with the hope of understanding the basic biochemical mechanisms involved.

Much of this early work was done by Klein and his group at Columbia.[2] They found that infusion of 0.5 mol racemic sodium lactate reliably precipitated panic attacks in 50 to 70 percent of patients who suffer clinical attacks, while doing so in less than 10 percent of normal controls. Klein's group also found that administration of tricyclic antidepressants resulted in a positive therapeutic response in panic disorder patients. Others have shown that panic attacks could be treated effectively by monoamine oxidase (MAO) inhibitors as well as by alprazolam, a triazolobenzodiazepine. If the panic attacks were thus successfully treated, they were also refractory to the effects of lactate infusion.

Soon after the Klein group experiments, Katerndahl made the following remarks concerning the problems with the lactate hypothesis:

> The increase in serum lactate produced by lactate infusion is minimal. Second, although the exercise-induced lactate response is increased in patients with cardiopulmonary disease, most do not have panic attacks. Finally, lactate is rapidly converted to bicarbonate in the body and the subsequent alkalosis may be responsible for the panic symptoms.[3]

In spite of these problems, the ability to instigate and alleviate panic attacks created intense interest in studying the pathophysiology of the disorder. The sodium lactate infusion experiments were the first to suggest the possibility that panic disorder was perhaps due to an internal or endogenous problem rather than a response to a purely external or exogenous stimulus. The lactate infusion response soon came to serve as a model for panic anxiety in the laboratory.[4]

Defective Biochemical Trigger Theory

The physiologic response during a panic attack is similar to that seen in the classic fight or flight anxiety response. The patient is prepared for action with an increase in heart rate, blood pressure, and respiratory rate. However, in panic attacks, these responses occur spontaneously without any external threat. Lactate's ability to precipitate panic attacks that resemble naturally occurring attacks both in symptoms and in pharmacological response led to multiple experiments to try to determine the mechanism for lactate's induction of panic symptoms and, subsequently, the biochemistry involved in panic disorder.

The biochemical trigger theory involves the idea that a basic vulnerability or underlying defect somewhere in the body's biochemistry makes the person more prone to unprovoked recurrent panic attacks. Herman and Deitch[5] liken this situation to a faulty smoke alarm that sounds when there is no smoke or fire in evidence.

Predisposing factors other than injection of sodium lactate may trigger panic attacks. Individuals who experience panic attacks are more sensitive to caffeine,[6] marijuana, yohimbine,[7] and carbon dioxide[8] than are normal controls. Herman and Deitch comment on the role of progesterone:

> The female hormone progesterone, released during the latter part of the menstrual cycle, is known to stimulate some of the same nervous system sites that are sensitive to caffeine and sodium lactate. Although progesterone has not been tested in people with panic disorder, some researchers speculate that this connection might help explain why panic attacks are twice as common in women as in men. (This 2 to 1 ratio, by the way, holds up across geographic, cultural, and socioeconomic boundaries.) It might also help explain why women with panic disorder tend to have more attacks during the premenstrual phase.[5]

The question remains as to whether the defective biochemical trigger mechanism involved is peripheral or central. Is the trigger due to a peripheral catecholamine surge or is it central (brain) in origin, involving noradrenergic stimulation? Liebowitz, Klein, et al. indicate, "Overall, our data suggest that no peripheral biochemical or physiological change serves as a trigger for lactate panic . . . peripheral catecholamine surge does not appear to be the mechanism by which lactate causes panic, although elevated plasma epinephrine may play a predisposing role."[9]

A search for a central physiologic basis for vulnerability has been associated with central sympathetic activation because of the similarity in physiologic changes seen in panic disorder. The investigations have centered on a possible instability of the locus ceruleus, the principal noradrenergic nucleus in the central nervous system that seems to help control emotional responses.

"The theory is that people with panic disorder have some basic metabolic defect that results in an excess of oversensitivity to certain chemical messengers in the blood. When these messengers penetrate the locus ceruleus, large quantities of norepinephrine are released, which in turn trigger the emotional and physical changes of panic."[5]

Liebowitz et al. suggest the following:

> If the locus ceruleus is involved in lactate-induced panic, two possibilities exist: 1) Panic patients suffer from central noradrenergic instability, and lactate infusions produce panic by CNS noradrenergic stimulation; or 2) panic patients suffer from some other psychobiological instability, which, when activated by lactate (or other stimuli), causes excessive input into and/or output from normally functioning central noradrenergic circuits. . . . Lactate induced panic attacks appear to be a primarily CNS phenomenon that has inconsistent peripheral sequelae. . . . Evidence of heightened central

noradrenergic activity is present during many but not all lactate-induced panic attacks; the significance of this remains to be established.[9]

Hyperventilation Theory

In 1983 Klein said, "Hyperventilation and related disorders of respiratory functions have been implicated in the pathogenesis of panic attacks. . . . Some believe that hyperventilation producing respiratory alkalosis produces panic, while others contend that hyperventilation is merely one of the secondary symptoms of a panic attack. . . . Our early results suggest that respiratory alkalosis is not a sufficient cause of panic attacks, but that carbon dioxide challenge may be panicogenic."[10]

Panic disorder patients frequently complain of dyspnea or shortness of breath. This may actually be hyperventilation. These patients seem to be in a state of chronic compensatory respiratory alkalosis. Studies have shown that carbon dioxide saturation, bicarbonate and phosphorous levels are all lower in panic disorder patients than in controls.[11] "This evidence suggests a chronic process of hyperventilation because, although carbon dioxide saturation is a very rapidly changing index, changes in bicarbonate and phosphorous take longer to develop."[12]

In 1985 Klein once again commented on the hyperventilation hypothesis.

> It has been demonstrated that patients suffering from this disorder regularly give very good evidence of being in a state of chronic compensated respiratory alkalosis. In this situation their pCO_2 is low, but the bicarbonate is also low, and therefore the pH is essentially

normal. The kidneys have compensated for the chronic blowing off of carbon dioxide. The question then arises, does this mean that hyperventilation causes panic attacks or does it mean that panic attacks cause hyperventilation? Because patients who suffer from panic attacks and have been asymptomatic on medication for an extended period demonstrate that their respiratory status returns to normal, it is suggested that the chronic compensated respiratory alkalosis is secondary to the panic experience. However, one could urge that it may be a vicious circle. The issue is still open.[13]

Ley takes another perspective.[14] He looks at the psychological profile and breathing behavior of agoraphobics who experience panic attacks. The agoraphobic is described as a sensitive person who has had a series of closely spaced stressors. The agoraphobic responds to heightened emotionality by overbreathing in the thoracic pattern via the mouth and is unaware of overbreathing and ignorant of the physical consequences.

Thus, Ley feels that extreme fear may be the consequence of an interaction between somatic and cognitive events that begins with the sudden awareness of unexpected bodily sensations, e.g., dyspnea, heart palpitations. His theory holds that the panic attack consists of a synergistic interaction between hyperventilation and fear. Ley therefore asserts that the traditional conception of the panic attack in agoraphobia may confuse the cause with the effect.

Current lab findings by Klein et al. suggest that, contrary to previous hypotheses, induction of metabolic alkalosis does not appear sufficient to cause panic during lactate infusion. These findings indicate that

> patients who panicked with lactate also did not develop greater alkalosis than nonpanicking patients, suggesting that no absolute pH threshold exists beyond which

clinically vulnerable patients automatically panic. Metabolic alkalosis in and of itself does not appear to be the mechanism by which lactate provokes panic. Also arguing against alkalosis as the mechanism for lactate-induced panic is the observation that room air hyperventilation sufficient to cause marked respiratory alkalosis did not cause panic attacks in the majority of patients who panicked with lactate.[15]

"Our data did not support induction of metabolic alkalosis as sufficient to cause panic during lactate infusion. Whether [it helps] to trigger panic attacks in combination with some unidentified variable, however, remains to be elucidated."[9]

Hypocalcemia Theory

Pitts and McClure,[1] in their landmark paper, observed that adding calcium to the lactate infusion considerably diminished the incidence and severity of resulting anxiety symptoms. This led to the hypothesis that lactate provoked panic by binding to ionized calcium at the surface of the excitable membranes.

Katerndahl[3] states that various panic symptoms, including dyspnea, dizziness, feelings of unreality, paresthesias, faintness, and trembling, can be attributed to hypocalcemia. He further states that "both lactate and alkalosis can cause relative hypocalcemia. Lactate complexes with calcium ions. When panic attacks are induced by lactate infusion, they can be alleviated by calcium infusion. However, more lactate would be required to produce significant hypocalcemia than could be expected to result from physiologic mechanisms. Alkalosis produces hypocalcemia by increasing the binding of calcium ions to albumin. When panic attacks are induced by bicarbonate infusion, free ionized calcium is reduced by 10 percent. Therefore, hypocalcemia has been considered a cause of panic attacks."[16]

Liebowitz et al., however, in their more recent paper, indicate that their studies seem to rule out lowered calcium levels as important in the lactate-induced panic attack.

> Pitts and McClure's finding that adding calcium to lactate infusion lowered the incidence of panic is compatible with but does not prove a panicogenic role for hypocalcemia. Adding calcium could have simply offset the effects of lactate on a noncalcium system. Our preliminary findings are that panickers, at the point of lactate-induced panic, do not have lower ionized calcium levels than comparably timed nonpanicking patients. This suggests that hypocalcemia per se does not cause panic attacks in clinically vulnerable patients. It is possible that lowered calcium, interacting with some other variable, is panicogenic.[2]

Thermostat Theory

In 1977 several groups discovered specific binding sites or diazepam (Valium) receptors in the brain. These sites are also called benzodiazepine receptors after the class of drugs which includes diazepam. This discovery of brain receptors for antianxiety drugs that were produced by the body opened the door to the "thermostat theory." This theory states that in panic disorder, the body's "thermostat" for regulating the production of these natural antianxiety substances is defective. These substances would ordinarily bind to receptors to alleviate anxiety.

It is unlikely that the brain developed diazepam

receptors in anticipation of Valium. Because Valium receptors are present, it is assumed that either endogenous natural Valium-like compounds or endogenous anti-Valiums exist in the human brain. It seems likely that these internal substances bind to the receptors to alleviate anxiety.

In this neurochemical process, "Benzodiazepine receptors modulate gamma-aminobutyric acid (GABA) systems. GABA is a major CNS (Central Nervous System) inhibitory transmitter. . . . One model for benzodiazepine action is as follows: GABA and the benzodiazepines bind to separate sites on a two-site receptor complex. Benzodiazepines may potentiate the action of GABA, thus increasing GABA effectiveness. . . . If anxiety causes excitation of certain neural circuits, GABA, through a feedback system, inhibits this excitation to reduce anxiety. Because there are benzodiazepine receptors in the brain, it can be hypothesized that benzodiazepine potentiates GABA at this locus and that these may be circuits that modulate anxiety."[17]

Meditation and other relaxation techniques as well as behavior modification therapy may relieve anxiety because they somehow stimulate the body's output of antianxiety chemicals.

Focal Brain Abnormality Theory

Positron emission tomography (PET) is a brain-imaging technique that safely provides quantitative, regional measurements of biochemical and physiological processes.[18] Recently, a research team using this technique may have identified a brain abnormality believed to cause panic attacks. They found that patients who are lactate-sensitive have abnormally higher oxygen metabolism, blood flow, and blood volume in the right side of the parahippocampal region. These patients also had an abnormally high whole brain oxygen metabolism and abnormal susceptibility to episodic hyperventilation (an acute respiratory alkalosis). These differences were found even when the patients were not suffering an active panic attack.

These data suggest increased brain cell activity in the right side. Thus, the researchers conclude, "We propose that the parahippocampal abnormality determines vulnerability to anxiety attacks. Furthermore, we propose that a triggering event, such as activation of noradrenergic projections to the hippocampal formation [the hippocampal formation receives abundant noradrenergic projections from the *locus ceruleus*], causes the abnormal region to initiate an anxiety attack by way of the septoamygdalar complex and its sequential projections."[19]

A triggering event such as stimulation by the neurochemicals created in the locus ceruleus (see the discussion of the defective biochemical trigger theory above), could cause the abnormal region to overreact and send distress signals to other parts of the brain that control the heart, breathing, and other involuntary systems. That, in turn, could cause heart palpitations, shortness of breath, and other symptoms of a panic attack.

These findings are important because they are among the first brain changes to be documented in such patients. They are also important because "the PET abnormalities . . . as well as the vulnerability to lactate with which they are associated, could reflect persistent markers of the illness. If these abnormalities are persistent, they could be evaluated as possible *genetic markers*.[19] (See the discussion of hereditary predisposition below.)

Psychological (Emotional) Theories

The psychological theorists look toward exogenous or external events and how they produce a panic disorder in the individual. Classically, psychological theorists see anxiety as an outward sign of internal conflict. Anxiety is a red flag signaling that certain emotions are trying to push upward from the unconscious. They deal with three basic predisposing factors in the etiology of panic disorder:

1. A history of childhood separation anxiety
2. Sudden loss of a significant person, particularly when there is an unresolved dependency conflict in the relationship
3. A series of stressful life events

Childhood Separation Anxiety

The history of panic disorder patients usually reveals that they had difficulty separating from their mother or mother substitute. They often were rather clinging children who did not want to leave home and resisted going to school. They often suffered a school phobia or refused to attend school. This is the most common form of separation anxiety disorder, characterized by the child's extreme anxiety at school and insistence on staying at home with the mother, often because of fear that something will happen to the mother during the separation.

A child's separation anxiety is often related to maternal anxiety about the child's welfare and her own adequacy as a mother, with a need for the child's approval. There is a 20 to 50 percent incidence of excessive childhood separation anxiety in the history of adult panic disorder patients, suggesting a pathophysiological link between pathological separation anxiety and adult panic attacks.[20]

Klein comments that many panic disorder patients have a childhood history of separation anxiety. He believes that it may be "related to a built-in mechanism that deals with separation anxiety of young infants that is a normal developmental process. This mechanism may go wrong, and it is conceivable that people with panic disorders or agoraphobia suffer a pathological deranged threshold that causes this mechanism to fire off when it is developmentally inappropriate."[10]

Sudden Loss of a Significant Person

The second psychological predisposing factor is that panic disorder is often precipitated by a loss. These patients often give a history of sudden loss of a significant other with whom they have an unresolved dependency conflict. The separation can result from the loss of a loved one through death (a spouse or parents) or a loss created by a breakup of a relationship or by moving to a new location. Even if a good history is taken, patients may not mention their loss until sometime later in therapy.

Often patients are not aware of their dependency needs. On the contrary, they see themselves as being independent. However, patients often speak of their loss in terms of their own need to have someone to whom they could turn for help, even if they never called upon that person. The loss of that person removed a significant psychological anchor.

A Series of Stressful Life Events

Stress also plays an important role in the etiology of panic disorder. "A recent National Institute of Mental Health study showed that more than 80 percent of people with panic disorder had experienced an unusually stressful life event not long before their first panic attack. In women, the stressful event is usually a major change in home or family life: a divorce or breakup of a relationship, loss or birth of a child (often, the birth of a second child). In men with panic disorder, the stressful event typically involves work: frequently a promotion or increased responsibility on the job."[5]

Panic disorder usually begins during late adolescence or early adulthood. The average age of onset is the 20s. During this time, we must deal with independence, career and relationship choices, and separation from our parents. It is often a time of adjustment from single or student life to full adult responsibilities. All of these issues can be complicated by unresolved dependency needs. For this reason, many have wondered whether panic disorder is related to the stress of this transitional period.

Before we can reach any conclusions about the etiology of panic disorder symptoms, we have to look at two other factors: The issues of *hereditary predisposition* and the *relationship of panic disorder to depression*. The relationship of panic disorder to depression was discussed in Chapter 2 under classification controversies.

Hereditary Predisposition

The role of heredity in the formation of panic attacks has not been settled. However, most studies show some correlation between family history and panic attacks. First-degree relatives of individuals with panic attacks show higher than expected rates of panic disorder. Crowe et al. have shown that "the disorder has a strong familial prevalence with rates in first-degree relatives reported to be as high as 30 percent, perhaps the highest of all psychiatric disorders."[21,22] A good history, once again, becomes important in diagnosis.

Studies with twins have also been used to demonstrate a genetic predisposition for panic disorder. For instance, it has been shown that monozygotic twin concordance exceeds that of dizygotic twins.[23] Surman et al. reported using genetic marking techniques, HLA (human leucocyte antigen), to provide evidence for a genetic susceptibility in panic disorder. They describe two sets of genotypic identical siblings, who were donor and recipient in a renal transplant, and who were all concordant for panic disorder.

However, the researchers issue a caution: "Because of the limited sample size, caution is necessary in interpreting these observations. . . . The possible association between panic disorder and the major histocompatibility gene complex invites more detailed studies with larger groups."[24]

In a recent linkage study of panic disorder, Crowe et al. showed that the transmission pattern within families is consistent with single-locus genetics. Preliminary findings implicate the long arm of chromosome 16.[25]

Etiologic Conclusions

We can now elaborate several biological hypotheses and point toward a biological trigger mechanism affecting some specific areas of the brain. We are also starting to see some psychological relationship between separation anxiety, loss, and stressful life events and panic disorder. Many studies show a correlation between family history and panic attacks and point toward an hereditary predisposition. Biological hypotheses and psychological theories when fully delineated may well be interrelated. Based on what is known at present, however, we may conclude the following:

Panic disorder is a result of specific stressful life events, most commonly separation or loss, in a person with a specific biologic (genetic or acquired) vulnerability.

The etiology of panic disorder still remains confusing and conflictual. Much work needs to be done. Investigation must include additional laboratory studies and longitudinal studies. As a psychiatric clinician, I feel that data obtained from the mental health worker in the field will also be valuable.

Mythology tells us that when Pan jumped out from the forest to scare and startle unwary travelers, he was motivated as much by mischief as by the wish to terrify. The confusion that still exists concerning the cause of panic disorder makes us wonder if Pan has not again been creating the noises in the forest and amusing himself with the chase.

6

Panic Disorder through the Life Cycle
A Longitudinal–Life History Approach

Just as the travelers of old did not know when Pan, the mythical god of the woods, would jump out at them causing anxiety and upheaval in their lives, our patients do not know when the cluster of psychological and somatic symptoms characteristic of his namesake, panic disorder, will appear or reappear in their lives. We are told that it is a disease of young people and most commonly appears during early adulthood, a time of heightened vulnerability, when many experience separation from home for the first time. It has a uniform unimodal age-of-onset distribution with a peak in the 20s. It rarely begins before the age of 12 or after the age of 40.[1] The mean age of onset in one study was 26.3 years.[2]

Clinically, panic disorder can be seen in various stages of life. Its presentation and course are really an unknown. Longitudinal studies are needed to track down its elusive path. Many articles on panic disorder end with the mandate that such studies are needed to fully understand the issues involved in this syndrome. For now, all we can do is look at the various stages of life and hypothesize about antecedent clues and possible signs that it will appear on the scene. Certain situations may create stress that will unlease panic symptoms in those with a specific biologic vulnerability.

Early Development/Childhood

Shakespeare's *The Tempest* tells us that "the past is prologue . . ."[3] to the future. This may well be the case with the constellation of symptoms that we call panic disorder. "Although panic disorder and agoraphobia with panic attacks usually begin in early adulthood,

117

they may be preceded by childhood anxiety or psychological trauma. Patients with panic disorder retrospectively report more childhood fears than do controls and often recall being anxious as children."[4] Raskin et al. found a higher rate of grossly disturbed childhood environments in patients with panic disorder than in patients with generalized anxiety disorder.[5]

Middle childhood or latency, from ages 6 to 11, is a period in which the child's attention and energies are focused primarily on continuing socialization and adjusting to the outside world, including school. Separation anxiety first becomes evident during this time and is one of the common psychiatric disorders during this period. It is also known as school phobia, school refusal, or "home-sickness."

Separation Anxiety

The basic feature of a separation anxiety disorder is the inability of the child to tolerate separations from the parental home, shown through a refusal to go to school, stay overnight with friends, attend camp, or at times being unable to stay comfortably in a room by themselves. At the same time, the child displays clinging behavior and shadowing of the parents. Typically, the picture begins with a number of somatic complaints which are vague and difficult to pinpoint. This is accompanied by considerable, obvious distress on the part of the child.[6]

"There may be a continuity between childhood and adult anxiety disorders, particularly between separation anxiety in childhood and agoraphobia in adulthood. In addition, there seems to be an aggregation of separation anxiety in children and panic disorder and agoraphobia in their parents."[7] Patients with agoraphobia with panic attacks have an increased rate of childhood separation anxiety, although the difference is seen primarily in women. Patients with panic disorder without agoraphobia do not report increased rates of separation experiences or separation anxiety as children suggesting that separation anxiety is more important for the subgroup of patients who develop agoraphobia. Clinically, patients with a history of separation anxiety show an earlier onset of panic attacks but no clear-cut difference in severity of illness.[8]

Klerman lists the following three ways that separation anxiety is linked to panic and agoraphobia in adults: (1) Agoraphobic adults report a greater than expected frequency of school phobia and separation anxiety as children. (2) School phobia and separation anxiety respond to tricyclic antidepressants, as do panic and agoraphobia. (3) Family studies indicate that children of parents with panic/agoraphobia have a higher incidence of school phobia and separation anxiety than the children of a matched control group.

He concludes: "These findings suggest that there is a relationship between adult agoraphobia and childhood separation anxiety, and that separation anxiety may be the childhood antecedent of adult panic attacks."[9] Panic disorder may represent a vestige of separation anxiety.

Panic disorder may also be related to behavioral inhibition in children. Jerome Kagan et al.[10] compared shy, quiet, socially avoidant children with those at the other behavioral extreme, who showed bold, fearless, talkative, and more spontaneous characteristics. Their evidence suggests that the shy child may have an inherited tendency to be hyperreactive physiologically, due to a lower threshold for limbic-hypothalamic arousal to unexpected environmental stress or change. Kagan and his associates feel that these distinctive behavioral and physiological patterns continue into adulthood and may contribute to the development of social anxiety, avoidance behavior, agoraphobic symptoms, and a greater propensity to develop panic attacks.

Adolescence/Young Adulthood

Separation is also a key developmental issue in adolescence. The teenage years are a period of explosive turbulence during which the individual deals with dependence and independence. This stage of life is a time of accelerated anatomic, physiologic, and emotional growth. Hormones trigger changes that will enable the teenager, through a series of tangential and experimental transitions, to cope with adult responsibilities.

Outwardly, the adolescent assumes an adult facade, based chiefly on imitation, while inside he or she is in a precarious state of limbo between childhood and adulthood. Emotional separation from the parents and the establishment of an independent way of handling life's problems is a task that is often fought by the adolescent through emotional outbursts, moodiness, and signs of depression.

In a search for personal identity, adolescents are often preoccupied with how others see them or how they perceive themselves. Since the adolescent stands midway between personal independence and continuing dependence on the parents, many emancipatory acts occur. Although adolescents experiment periodically with various modes of self-expression, a stable personality structure will eventually form.[11]

Adolescence proper is a struggle between independence and dependence as the individual disengages from early object ties. In late adolescence, selective life tasks acquire shape through their consolidation of social roles and identifications. However, the total achievement still lacks harmony.

Young adulthood further refines this process. It is a period of transition and increased responsibility. In the United States today, the end of adolescence is difficult to pinpoint, due to changing socioeconomic developments. The unemployed as well as the employed young adult may stay in the parental home. The youthful technological or professional trainee may have to remain financially dependent on parents well into the twenties.

"The transition from adolescence is marked by an intervening phase, postadolescence, which can be claimed rightfully by both . . ."[12] During this phase, integration comes about gradually as the individual moves away from home for the first time, establishes himself in the job market, activates a social role, makes significant interpersonal choices, perhaps becomes a parent, and takes on additional responsibilities of adult life. Panic disorder usually begins in late adolescence or early adulthood, a time of choices, transition, and separation. This author wonders if panic disorder is not related to the stress of this transitional period.

Clinical Vignette: Jody

The following vignette illustrates a case of panic disorder that appeared for the first time during young adulthood. Jody was 26 years old and had been married for three years. She had had her first child prematurely in April. The child remained in "intensive care" for three weeks before she could be taken home. The patient had her first panic attack on the day of her daughter's christening. As she drove home from the church, she suddenly couldn't swallow, was short of breath, felt dizzy, had hot and cold flashes, palpitations, and stomach pain. She was scared. "I felt it was going to take over. I thought I would lose my mind and someone would come and lock me up because I was crazy." The attack only lasted ten minutes but returned the next week while she was alone at home with the baby. The attacks increased in frequency to three to four per day.

There was no prior history of psychiatric treatment or hospitalization. Family history showed a maternal grandmother who had "nervous problems." Psychotherapy revealed ambivalent feelings and some regrets about the responsibility of parenthood. "I thought it would be so perfect. There's so much responsibility. I have to do the right thing. She's all mine. I'm the sole person responsible for her. I love her, but sometimes, I feel I want out. Before this, life was always a party. I enjoyed my work and did it well. I enjoyed being with people and going out to lunch. Now, I'm stuck in and secluded."

Middle Age

Stress, particularly that which threatens or changes a person's emotional security, is an important factor in the etiology of panic disorder. Middle age, a period of change and crisis for both men and women, can certainly meet these criteria. The change of life with its waning ovarian function and the cessation of menses is a universal phenomenon. Many cultures adhere to an elaborate mythology that suggests that women go crazy at the change of life. Menopause is not a sickness, but rather a normal process that ushers in a phase that lasts to the end of a woman's life. The changes occur because of physical, hormonal, and chemical rebalancing.

Much of the anxiety associated with the change of life is not related to its physiologic effects, but to the deep-rooted negative attitudes Americans have toward aging. Outside pressures, such as parents growing old and sick, children leaving home, and careers and relationships that are no longer satisfying tend to deepen the tensions associated with the change of life.

Middle age is a time of reassessment for men as well as women. They too are forced to come to terms with the fact that they are getting older. Just as women go through the change of life, men may experience, at approximately the same age, a psychologic "male menopause" marked by depression, a sense of frustration, disillusionment with old goals, and a sudden awareness that "time is running out."

These feelings, if recognized and understood, may motivate the middle-aged man to adopt new, more productive, creative, and satisfying living patterns. Without this recognition, the individual may deal with the crisis by just changing everything around him. For instance, he may suddenly plunge into sexual escapades with younger women, change jobs, try cosmetic surgery, or experiment with drugs in an attempt to forget or ignore what he is experiencing.[13]

The following clinical vignette will illustrate how

change and loss in middle age, in this case, reactivating the unresolved loss of a parent in adolescence, appears to have precipitated panic disorder.

Clinical Vignette: Marie

Marie, 43 years old and divorced, was referred to me by her family physician due to anxiety and stress. She related that she had been under much job tension. Approximately 10 months before she was hospitalized for possible appendicitis, which was diagnosed as Crohn's disease (regional enteritis). After this, she was quite irritable at work, her job attendance was sporadic, and within three months she took a better job offer at a rival company.

Her new job situation was not an improvement. From the beginning, she felt under pressure, was "nervous," and had difficulty sleeping. In June, she was forced to take on additional responsibility when her boss became ill. At the beginning of July, her boss died, leaving her with the total responsibility of the office.

In August she was hospitalized for what she termed a "stress attack." Her Crohn's disease flared up, her blood pressure was elevated, and she complained of headaches. She said that she felt "nervous" and tearful.

Marie's panic attacks had begun, but remained undiagnosed for several weeks. Her family physician questioned her closely and learned that during these attacks, her palms sweated, her chest tightened, she was dizzy, her heart raced, and she felt shaky inside. She was also restless, fearful, and afraid that something terrible was going to happen to her. Psychiatric referral followed.

During our initial sessions, I learned that she had been married twice and was now divorced for the past 10 years. She had an 18-year-old daughter, who had just started college out of town. The patient's mother was living. Her father had died when she was 18. Marie was the youngest of three siblings and the only female. She currently had a boyfriend, with whom she was annoyed because he frequently went away on business.

After confirming the diagnosis of panic disorder, I suggested a trial of medication. She was not compliant. On her second visit, she stated that she preferred to do without medication. Our first four sessions were uneventful. She said that she was feeling more in control and having less frequent attacks. She seemed to be responding to education, reassurance, supportive responses, and some ventilation of her frustrating situation.

After canceling the next session, she showed up a week later carrying the book, *How to Survive the Loss of a Love*. As I am apt to do, I asked her about the book, how she had chosen to read it, and if it related to her. "I just picked it up off the bookstore shelf," she said.

With some encouragement, she started to talk about the various losses that she had recently experienced. Slowly, she told me how she missed her friends from her other job. She went on to tell me about her feelings after her first attack of Crohn's disease.

"It frightened me. I felt I was getting older. My whole life shifted." She told me for the first time that just prior to changing jobs, she had been attacked when someone broke into her house. She told me about a recent argument with her boyfriend over his not fulfilling her needs.

Suddenly, she was talking about her father. "He

died twenty-four years ago. It is only recently that I
have started to deal with his death. I was the only girl—
the baby of the family. We were always close. He always did things for me. I always knew he was there if I
needed him. My mother is old and sickly. I have this
fear that something will happen. My daughter is away
at college. I am alone."

She started to cry softly and related the following
experience that she had had in acting class several
months before her first panic attack. "They had us lie
on the floor with the lights out. We had to fantasize that
we were playing in a park with friends and having fun.
All of a sudden, the friends leave and we are alone and
afraid. A man walks up with a bunch of beautiful bal-
loons. As we reach to take them, it is our father and he
slaps our hands. We run home to our family for support
and comfort.

"Suddenly, I was crying. I wanted to run out of the
room. No one knew what was wrong with me. I was
flooded with memories of my father. He would never
have slapped my hand. At home, my father wasn't
there anymore. Mother was sick and would soon be out
of my life. I cried and cried. I finally realized that Dad
was really dead. I felt all alone."

Thus, with one swoop of emotion, this terribly independent, overly conscientious woman expressed her
fear, exposed her human vulnerability, ventilated her
multiple recent losses, and admitted for perhaps the
first time that she too had dependency needs. Somehow, she started to feel whole again and felt more comfortable with her adult role. She stayed in therapy for
three months.

Two months later she wrote to me.

"First let me thank you for all of the positive
growth I have received while under your care . . . I feel

as though I can [now] walk this road with confidence and self-assurance, from this point on. Things don't look as desperate as they did when we first met. . . . Instead of looking up at them and seeing mountains . . . I find myself looking down at them and seeing simply stepping stones.

"As for my worry and what-have-you concerning my daughter going away to college, well, she will be just fine. She even made the dean's list. All of that worry for nothing! She is adjusting beautifully and now, seeing her do so well, I rest that I will do just fine with my new life also. . . . I know I'm gonna make it now and not all alone but also with the help of others. That's a very nice feeling."

She had not had another panic attack.

Clinical Vignette: Russ

Russ's entire personality stressed his desire to appear manly and be totally independent. Completely unaware of his dependency needs, he nevertheless overcompensated for them. He worked in construction and prided himself on being the "number one guy," who could physically outperform his men. He had little patience for vulnerability in himself or others. At age 53, he was having trouble maintaining his facade.

He had experienced little contact with his father, a merchant seaman, who was often away. The patient's mother was 16 when he was born. She abandoned him to the care of his grandmother two years later. His grandmother died suddenly when he was 16. This was a severe second loss. Russ, however, saw himself as having been on his own since age 10.

The patient married in his late twenties after numerous sexual encounters. There were five children, born one year apart. He tended to be overprotective but was a caring and involved father. He was a good provider and prided himself on being able to support his family in spite of layoffs during the winter months. At age 32, he learned that his wife had had an affair. To make matters worse, it happened during one of these layoffs.

Although angry, he feared confronting her. Deep inside, he was afraid that she would leave him. He tried to sweep his feelings under the rug. He became overly anxious and irritable and developed an overpowering fear of death. In the spring, he started to have periodic attacks that seemed to confirm his fear. During these episodes, his heart raced and he trembled inside. He felt weak and had difficulty getting his breath. His stomach hurt and he often had diarrhea.

At first, he was reluctant to go for help, feeling that he should be able to handle it himself. However, he was aware of the violent anger he felt inside and feared that he would lose control during one of the attacks. He was restless and agitated. When his attacks started to interfere with his work, he finally spoke to his physician. Psychiatric hospitalization was recommended and the patient complied.

His psychiatrist realized that Russ was suffering from anxiety, but did not really fully understand his symptoms. He was treated with large doses of chlorpromazine, which made him feel "groggy" and "out of it." He was also offered some psychotherapy. Although very private at first, he gradually shared some of his anger and frustration. He even spoke, for the first time, about the fact that his mother had abandoned him. What bothered him most was her failure to make any attempt to contact him and offer an explanation for her behavior. This issue was tremendously emotionally charged. After four weeks of hospitalization, feeling calmer and more in control, he was released to return to the care of his family physician.

This author met Russ some 20 years later. His attacks had returned. His physical symptoms were similar to those that he had experienced before. He had gotten to the point that he was afraid to drive or go long distances, anticipating that he would have another attack. He was very upset but did not like his "strong feelings." He felt that they made him "weak." He wanted no part of what was happening to him and feared loss of control.

Russ had recently undergone a cardiac workup, including a stress test, which showed no evidence of cardiac ischemia or coronary vascular disease. His blood pressure was moderately elevated and he had an inguinal hernia. Due to his anxiety and multiple unsubstantiated physical complaints, he was referred for psychiatric evaluation by his internist.

History revealed multiple recent stresses in his life. His children were leaving home. There were job and financial pressures. He noted physical signs of aging and did not like them at all. At times, he was having trouble "making his body perform," sexually and at work.

Russ's thoughts predominantly involved his job. He reported that he was normally able to control things at work and was respected by his men. However, he was beginning to feel less in control and felt that some of the "young bucks" were starting to question his orders and authority. In our second session, he revealed that his mother had been trying to make contact with him after years of avoidance and silence.

The Geriatric Years

The geriatric years are another phase of life that can be extremely stressful for some. "As people grow old, they often experience pain and frustration born of their own difficulties in dealing with change and the accentuation of their own personality traits. For some, work or family is the only investment they have made in life. When physical illness and a lowered economic status are added, they will feel helpless and useless. . . ."[13] Physical, psychosocial, economic, and interpersonal changes can produce multiple losses and tremendous fluctuations in security.

"Forgetfulness and the diminution of their cognitive ability produce psychologic losses. Physical and physiologic losses follow changes in health, strength, and appearance. Hearing and visual defects appear to reinforce or trigger the development of paranoid symptoms. A reduced income and property losses are economic losses. Social losses include a possible change in prestige, status, and respect. Changes in sexual ability also may be perceived as a loss. The deaths of family members and friends provide additional interpersonal losses."[13]

"A stumbling block to a realistic understanding of the elderly is the misconception that senility is the only problem of the aged. . . . When many think of the elderly, a confused, forgetful, childlike person comes to mind. However, senility is found in only approximately 15 percent of the people who live past the age of 65—a small minority. The elderly are prone to a range of emotional problems. These disorders include neurotic symptoms, personality disorders, and even psychoses. Drug and alcohol abuse are often hidden disorders.[12] Panic disorder is also possible. In the over-65 age group, it is present only about one-twelfth as often as in the 25 to 44 age group.[14] Perhaps the change and loss of this period are factors in its presentation during this stage of life.

Clinical Vignette: Mrs. Elliot

The following vignette will illustrate some of these points. Mrs. Elliot was 68 years old. Her initial sessions concentrated on her physical symptoms and her responsibilities for taking care of others. When asked about recent stress, she mentioned that she had been hospitalized earlier that year for hypertension. During this time, her brother had died. Over the course of the next few sessions, the list grew. She had always envisioned that this time of her life would be tranquil and happy. The last four years had instead been a traumatic time of continuous change and unhappiness.

Four years ago, her husband had suffered a coronary and underwent bypass surgery. Two years ago, he had retired. A year ago, her daughter, whom she described as being very supportive, moved out of town. They used to live five minutes apart. Prior to his death, the patient's brother had lived with and cared for their mother. The patient was concerned that her mother now lived alone. She reported that her mother was a strong, healthy woman, who had cared for her children alone after the death of her husband, when the patient was age 16. Recently, her health was declining and she needed additional care due to escalating physical problems. An older sister was ill.

Several sessions later, the patient also mentioned that her husband had been in an automobile accident three months before. "He wasn't hurt. He is fine, but he could have been killed." Soon thereafter, her panic attacks, which she had been experiencing for several years, escalated. We will hear more about Mrs. Elliot in the next chapter.

7

Treatment
The Initial Phase—Reassurance and Education

Clinical Vignette Continued

For several years, Mrs. Elliot had suffered from anxiety attacks that would wake her out of a sound sleep. During the last 3–4 months, they had increased in frequency and intensity, and she had started to experience them during the day. During an attack, she felt restless, hyperventilated, and experienced a terrible feeling that she could not describe. She also spoke of having the sensation of feeling her blood rushing to her head.

Further probing indicated that at these times she also had palpitations, shortness of breath, an urge to urinate, and felt dizzy and weak. She sweated profusely and had hot flushes. Sometimes, during an attack, she had diarrhea, heartburn, a lump in her throat. She was afraid she would lose control. "It is horrible. The worst part is being so scared. Mentally, I think I am losing it." She ended by telling me that she could only wish these symptoms on Hitler.

Mrs. Elliot is not unique in her description of the subjective horrors of a panic attack. Most patients describe the experience as being a frightening living hell. Often their efforts in trying to find solutions to their problem only add to their turmoil and sense of frustration. Many have been to emergency rooms, family physicians, and multiple specialists, only to be told that there is nothing physically wrong to account for their symptoms. For some, this only reinforces their fears that they have indeed gone crazy. They often anticipate further humiliation, hopelessness, and rejection as they continue from doctor to doctor.

The Therapeutic Aspects of Diagnosis

It can indeed be a very fragile and emotionally battered individual that comes to your office for evaluation. An adequate treatment plan for panic disorder must therefore comprise many specific aspects. The first of course is to *make the diagnosis* and share it confidently and directly with the patient. As the first person to encounter the patient with some understanding of his or her symptoms, you are in a unique position to do an enormous therapeutic service by giving them a clear, precise definition of their illness and once and for all showing them that their symptoms have meaning. Let them know that it is only since 1980 that panic disorder has a name and that it is only during this decade that even psychiatry is beginning to understand this malady.

Making the diagnosis requires that you think about and elicit specific information. This will also require that you take into consideration the differential diagnosis issues mentioned in Chapter 4. Start out by listening carefully to both the feeling tone and the facts that they present in their initial chief complaint. Ask questions and look for the pieces of the puzzle that they have forgotten to include. Review all information about prior physical evaluations, special tests, and consultations. Do a medical history by system review. Suggest any additional physical modalities or tests that you feel will be helpful in making a differential diagnosis. Review all medications taken for either physical or emotional reasons.

Take a careful psychiatric history, including a mental status examination. Ask about prior psychiatric treatment or hospitalization. Ask about drug or alcohol use. Particularly question the history of the panic symptoms and the patient's description of their attacks. Usually, just giving the patient a definition of panic disorder and reviewing the common symptoms that accompany the attacks can serve to make them feel that they are not unique or alone.

I often read them this information from a pre-printed card. This helps me draw out missing symptoms. This technique also allows me to comment that they could not be the only one with this disorder, if I could have it printed on a card. Ask about stressful events, including losses and other life changes. Ask about the people in their life. These questions will help lay the groundwork for further discussions later.

The hope is that just putting together all of the information gleaned from the above evaluation will enable you either to rule out or definitely make the diagnosis of panic disorder. Just giving their complaints a name may do much to allay their fears, gain their cooperation, and reduce their anxiety. "Patients are relieved to know that they have a well-defined and easily identifiable syndrome, which is both understandable and treatable."[1] Like many, Mrs. Elliot responded to this information by relaxing a little and telling me that she felt so good that her disorder was no longer such an unknown. For her, the diagnosis had particular value. She felt that it validated her and proved that she was not a hypochondriac or a figure of ridicule.

Establishing Rapport

"Although the awareness of panic disorder as a separate diagnostic entity has allowed more accurate diagnosis, its treatment is still not an exact science. A physician's rapport with the patient is paramount, particularly because of the initial belief that the disorder must have a physical cause. Patients often consult many other physicians in an effort to obtain relief, and may be skeptical of a treatment plan based on a psychological premise,"[2] as well as a theory of physical vulnerability. Although it is difficult to separate the different aspects of the initial phase of treatment of the panic patient, *establishing rapport* is usually essential to effective treatment.

Treat the patient as an adult. Taking patients seriously may help mitigate their sense of helplessness and reestablish their sense of worth. You may be the first to do this. Just giving them the feeling that you think they are reasonable and likable people and not an annoyance may help. Share any positive feelings that you have about their personality, abilities, or special areas of interest that you notice during the initial interview.

For some time past they may have been seen as manipulative, frustrating, and difficult. Your view of them will mean a lot. Mrs. Elliot, for instance, was referred by her family physician. He had conscientiously used all of his knowledge and skill to solve this patient's diagnostic riddle. He had run multiple tests, had given her several anxiolytic agents, and had even given her a trial on two antidepressants at low doses. When he called me, he was ready to pull his hair out of his head due to her constant demands for relief from her bothersome symptoms.

Offering Reassurance

The next beneficial ploy is to offer reassurance in large doses. Explain anxiety and panic to them so that they may understand their various ramifications. Let them know what is possible and what is not. This knowledge will help mitigate their fears and fantasies. For instance, the patient should be given constant reinforcement that although the anxiety attacks are quite scary, they are self-limiting, will pass, and will not last forever. They already know this from their own experience, but somehow do not use it to help themselves. Your verbalizing this one small piece of information may help them get through their next attack without so much fear or trepidation.

Second, tell them that they will *not* die. Although a panic attack feels as if the end is near, *nobody ever died just from anxiety*. Although somewhat simplistic, they need to hear this from you. Verify for them that they are not going crazy or going out of their mind. So many before you may have inadvertently played into this fear.

Deal with the issue of control. Tell them that they are definitely *not* losing control. For many, it is really quite the opposite. Panic patients are often people who overvalue control, and fear the unknown. This may be a good time to start to tease out other examples that may show this to be a recurrent problem.

Lastly, it is helpful to reassure them that their symptoms are not a sign of weakness, failure, childishness, overdependency, or other anticipated fears of being less than perfect. This will also help alleviate any guilt feelings that they may have been harboring because they felt that they "should" have been able to stop or control their attacks. Guilt may also be a factor here in other ways. Tell them that the disorder is not their fault and was not caused by anything that they did. Make sure that they know that they do not have to feel guilty or punish themselves.

Education

Aside from diagnostic information, it is also helpful to educate panic patients about their disorder. Talk to them about anxiety, its meaning, and its etiology. Quote them a few statistics so that they know that they are not alone. Tell them about some of the panic disorder research, particularly the results of the positron emission tomography studies, that I spoke of in Chapter 5.

Explain that although they have been going through various stresses in their life, they may also have a specific physical vulnerability. Tell them that panic disorder may have an hereditary predisposition, particularly if you discover a family history of anxiety or depression.

Included here can be some information about possible complications. This will necessitate teaching them some new vocabulary. Urge your patient to confront and minimize secondary avoidance behavior and not allow phobias to develop. It is helpful to define these terms so that everyone is talking the same language. Point out that if they do not fight against the development of agoraphobia, then they will further complicate their situation in that they will then have *two* problems to handle. The secondary avoidance behavior may often be harder to treat and obliterate than the primary panic symptoms.

To prevent the phobias that can be complications of panic disorder, the clinician should clearly and forcefully tell the patient that the situation or place (car, supermarket, bridge, and so forth) that they associate with the panic attack was not the *cause* of their emotional response. *It is only a place where an unpleasant experience occurred.* The same panic attack may or may not have come out of the blue to overwhelm them where ever they were. Patients should be told that *avoiding such places only exacerbates their problems,* and that their constant *anticipation is the real source of the problem.*

Urge them not to limit their activities or life-style. Tell them, "There is no association between the attack and where you happen to be or what you are doing. It would have happened even if your were at home. If an attack occurs, just deal with it wherever you are. You now have new tools and ammunition to help you cope."

Some will still lament that they feel more secure if they are at home, or with a friendly, strong person. Acknowledge that you can understand these feelings; but tell them that neither people nor places really affect the production of anxiety attacks. In some cases, you may allow them this crutch for a short time. However, gradually wean them off and push them to confront their fears alone. Most of all, encourage them to continue to be active and not avoid places or situations that they fear will trigger an attack.

They need to be told about the concept of anticipatory anxiety and reassured that it is a common manifestation. It can often precede attacks or be a residual component. It is often the last symptom to disappear. Even after she was panic-free for some time, Mrs. Elliot spoke of being "a little tense" that she would have another attack. However, experiencing this form of anxiety does not mean that they are going to have an attack. They need to separate these two issues that they have placed in an equation that does not equate.

Educate the patient about the various treatment options. Tell them that although there are no guarantees and that you have no magic wand, there are several ways that you can help them. Tell them that there are various issues that you feel it will be important to discuss in therapy. Let them know that there are several available medications that will possibly be helpful. By reviewing these alternatives and then setting up a definite treatment plan, you will break up their cycle of hopelessness that has followed their clinical course up to now.

Self-Help Techniques

This initial phase of treatment is a good time to share with the patient some ways that they can help themselves. This begins to set the scene for an attitude of fostering independence that may take on great importance later in therapy. "Throughout the treatment of panic disorder, independence should be stressed, and the patient should be encouraged to take steps toward emotional maturation. Many behavioral and emotional strategies can help patients achieve this goal and should be encouraged."[2]

Some behavioral techniques, useful with general anxiety, may also be helpful here. They are as follows. "During panic attacks, many patients tend to withdraw. They should be encouraged to not be alone—to call someone on the telephone or seek out supportive companionship. Physical touch is also important—a hug may help patients relax . . . . Patients may also find that writing down their feelings in a diary can help allay anxiety."[2] Generally, you should encourage behavior that helps develop a new independent and mature life-style.

Some emotional strategies for dealing with anxiety can also be related to patients. Some of these, including how to deal with feelings of fear, loss of control and guilt, have already been suggested under the section on establishing rapport. To these I would add, encouraging patients to own up to their underlying problems and take responsibility for their actions.

This will become easier as they learn more about themselves in therapy. For now, they are probably so overwhelmed by the intense feelings and limitations imposed by the panic disorder symptoms that they cannot see the forest for the trees. Although they should learn to take responsibility for their actions, they should be advised to avoid perfectionism, which is common to patients with anxiety attacks.

There are other behaviors that you may wish to encourage them to reduce, particularly in reference to other people. "They should not try to please everyone or to live up to impossible expectations—both of which tend to increase stress. Physicians should try to help them avoid becoming frustrated with others for not being more supportive or sympathetic, by explaining that they may appear to be functioning better than they realize."[2]

How Can Family Members and Friends Help?

The support network around the patient is very important to their recovery. Often people may be very frustrated and upset by the patient's symptoms and behavior and ask to talk to you. In other cases, you may wish to encourage one or two of them to accompany the patient to treatment. Regardless of how they arrive, with the patient's permission, take the opportunity to answer their questions, educate them about the illness, and gain their constructive help. There are at least five things that they can do to help.

They can *offer emotional support*. "Family members and friends . . . should be advised to be supportive and understanding and to verbalize their caring—not just their feelings of frustration and helplessness. They should be helped to understand that the patient's feelings are very real and painful and that the behavior is not childish."[2] Family and friends should not minimize the situation, convey that they think less of the person because of this problem, or put the person down. *Acceptance* is important.

Using their new fund of information gleaned in your office, they too can *reassure and educate* their loved ones that the anxiety will pass, that they are not dying, losing control, or going crazy. They can *encourage independence*. Although they should let the patient know that they are available and willing to be supportive, they should also help them to deal with the anxiety in a problem-solving manner on their own.

They can also *encourage the patient to seek or continue with psychiatric help*, if self-help measures are unsuccessful or if the disorder is interfering with their total functioning. Tell them, however, not to badger the patient. Instead tell them to communicate that they care, understand, and are concerned. Thus, it is important that you educate significant others about the different aspects of panic disorder. An aware and knowledgeable support person can be a tremendous adjunct to treatment and a wonderful source of encouragement for your patient.

Clinical Vignette: Jim and Julie

The following vignette will illustrate an example where this support and understanding was not available, causing a tremendous rift in a relationship. Jim had been having anxiety attacks for 3–4 years when he first came to my office.

He described them as "terrified states" during which he had pains in his chest, palpitations, headaches, and shook inside. He felt fearful, restless, and keyed up and wanted to hide under the bed or sit huddled up on the bathroom floor. He was sure he was losing control. Recently, they had become more frequent causing him to avoid situations where he had experienced an attack, such as the movies.

His second complaint involved his marital situation. He had been married for three years and had a two-year-old daughter. Jim and his wife, Julie, had problems in communication, differences in personality style, and many unfulfilled needs. He complained that his wife chastised him for his panic attacks and told him that he should stop being a baby. He complained that she was not supportive or caring and was a "mommy's girl," who spent much of her time with her mother.

He brought me a dream that involved his having trouble carrying a large, heavy trash bag. In the dream, his wife just stands by and doesn't offer to help. He responds by putting his head down in shame. In a subsequent session, he revealed that he had a "case of the guilts" for having had a "one-night stand" several months ago.

History revealed that his parents had separated when he was in elementary school. He described his mother as a hardworking independent woman who was an alcoholic. His father was seen as a very critical man, who was never around, and could never be pleased. He revealed that he had not spoken to his father in many years. Three months ago, his father had moved back to the Philadelphia area. He had seen him once. During this visit, the man expressed disappointment that the patient had dropped out of school.

At my request, the patient's wife, Julie, came to the office to talk. My efforts were aimed at explaining the patient's disorder and trying to glean some understanding of the relationship from her point of view. She came across as lonely, unhappy, angry, and depressed. She stated that she did not want to try and work with the relationship. During the next four months, she left on two occasions, taking the child with her. The patient agonized over whether she would return.

In therapy he dealt with issues of security, dependency, and his feelings of guilt, anger, and hurt. He also dealt with his feelings about his parents, particularly his father. On one occasion, he asked his father for a loan to put a down payment on a house. He was turned down.

His treatment included chemotherapy, as well as individual and group psychotherapy. With therapy, the patient became more assertive, his work performance improved, and things seemed to be going better at home. Although his anxiety did not disappear completely, his panic attacks diminished greatly in frequency and intensity. He stopped treatment after eight and one-half months because he felt that things were going OK. I did not hear from Jim for five years. He recently called to tell me that he was seeking a divorce.

Making Human but Expert Contact

During the initial evaluation period, the clinician needs to show that he is concerned and yet competent and knowledgeable enough to deal with the presenting symptoms. The panic disorder patient has been through the mill, having usually visited many physicians and tried to obtain information and relief in many different ways. They will, to say the least, have mixed feelings about going to yet another professional about their problem.

Just as you are learning about the patient, he or she is also evaluating you. They want to know that you understand them. They must also feel comfortable talking and sharing personal information with you. Your words, manner, and behavior will set the tone for the therapy to come. In order to establish trust, you must make contact with the patient in a very human but expert way.

As noted, your goals during this initial phase of treatment need to include making a definite diagnosis and establishing rapport. During this time, you must also offer reassurance about the limits of their disorder and help reestablish their emotional equilibrium. Reduce feelings of guilt, if they are a factor. Patients need to know that they are adequate adults who are not going crazy, or losing control. You must educate them about the meaning of their symptoms and their possible complications. Explain the alternatives for treatment of panic disorder to both the patient and significant others.

Finally, you need to set up a clear, individualized treatment plan and share it with the patient. In doing this, be sure that you indicate that the plan is not written in stone and can be changed if necessary. The initial phase of therapy, that incorporates all of these elements, can offer much benefit. If you are successful in this task, your patient will leave the office feeling relieved, encouraged, pleased and, most important of all, less anxious.

8

Treatment
Individual Psychotherapy

Clinical Vignette: Joyce

Joyce would be 40 years old in three months. She felt jumpy, irritable, and alone. She had remarried ten months ago, but complained that she did not "feel together as husband and wife." Her first husband had walked out on her three years ago after 15 years of marriage. She described him as her strength and her security. He had just remarried. To make matters worse, her parents had recently retired and moved to South Carolina. She said that she felt unsettled, not connected, and vulnerable.

One month prior to our first visit, she started to have daily attacks of anxiety that lasted approximately 20 minutes. At these times, she was "nervous," hyperventilated, felt weak, was short of breath, had a smothering sensation and slight chest pain, had difficulty swallowing, felt nauseated, and felt hot and cold.

During the attacks, she also experienced a fear of losing control. She related that her father was "nervous" and that her sister also had "anxiety attacks."

During weekly individual psychotherapy, Joyce was helped to get a clearer and more objective picture of her two husbands. Gradually, she was able to see that, although her present husband's personality was less intense, he could be understanding. Over time, he showed her that he could be there for her, although he required that she be more responsible.

As she started to separate emotionally from her first husband, her trust level increased, and she allowed herself to be closer to her present spouse. She was able to deal with her anger that there had been people in her life who had left her for various reasons, although she had been faithful and supportive.

151

A therapeutic breakthrough came after she spent several summer weeks visiting with her parents in South Carolina. She was amazed to observe how overprotective and anxious they were. She could see how they had transmitted their anxiety to their children. "I was always Daddy's little girl. For my mother, everything was black or white. There was only one way to do everything. I guess I always wanted an environment that was as perfect as hers seemed."

During our last session, Joyce commented on how different her world now was. "I always saw myself in this 'perfect little world' . . . I set my expectations too high . . . I saw Jim [first husband] as my security. He took care of everything. Now I have a more active role in my marriage and my life."

Weekly individual psychotherapy sessions were an integral part of Joyce's treatment plan. "Psychotherapy is the treatment, by psychological means, of problems of an emotional nature in which a trained person deliberately establishes a professional relationship with the patient with the object (1) of removing, modifying, or retarding existing symptoms, (2) of mediating disturbed patterns of behavior, and (3) of promoting positive personality growth and development."[1]

The Psychiatric History: The Initial Phase of Psychotherapy

The psychiatric history is the crucial first phase of psychotherapy. Here the clinician obtains important information allowing him to start to understand the patient as a person. During this time, he establishes rapport to promote the development of a constructive therapeutic relationship. Additional purposes of the psychiatric history is to comprehend the patient's personal development, understand the environment in which it occurred, learn the significance of the principle figures in that environment, and understand the patient's adaptive techniques and defense mechanisms.

The following information on the psychiatric history has been selected with particular emphasis on interviewing the patient whom you suspect of having panic disorder.

History of psychiatric treatment or hospitalization is important to rule out other psychiatric illnesses that show anxiety symptoms and help with the differential diagnosis of panic.

Family history of mental illness is important because of the suspected genetic/familial predisposition of panic disorder. The patient should be questioned about family members who have shown problems with anxiety, depression, or alcoholism.

The longitudinal or personal history may give some clues of premorbid issues involved in the panic-prone patient. Ask about the patient's reaction to school, school phobias, or separation anxiety during childhood. In the adolescent period listen for difficulties in separation. In young adulthood, question whose idea it was for them to move from the parental home and their reaction to the move. Look for evidences of emotional crises and difficulties.

The Mental Status Examination

All of the above questions lead into and often answer some of the questions asked in the mental status examination. The mental status exam is to the psychiatrist what auscultation, percussion, and palpation are to the internist. Many of the questions asked here will aid with differential diagnosis. (See Chapter 4 on Differential Diagnosis.)

1. General appearance, manner, and attitude. (Patients with panic disorder may appear calm during interview.)
2. Consciousness, including orientation as to time, place, and person.
3. Apperception-perception as modified by one's own emotions, memories, and biases.
4. Affectivity and mood. (Fear or apprehension suggest anxiety.)
5. Conation and motor aspects of behavior.
6. Associations and stream of thought.
7. Thought life and mental trend including delusions (false beliefs). (Ask about phobias, obsessions, compulsions, and excessive fears or bodily preoccupation.)
8. Perception, including auditory and visual hallucinations.
9. Memory, both recent and remote. (Retention and recall—digit span is impaired in extremely anxious patients.)
10. Fund of information. (Intellectual function is intact in patients with anxiety disorders.)
11. Judgment. (The ability to compare facts or ideas, to understand their relations, and to draw correct conclusions from them).
12. Insight (the extent to which a patient is aware that he is ill). (Anxiety patients are often unwilling to accept an emotional explanation for their physical condition.)

Areas to Explore and Understand in Therapy

The psychiatric history and mental status examination helps the clinician to make a definitive diagnosis and also then begin the process of learning about the patient. This process is in itself therapeutic as pieces of information start to come together and connections are made.

In therapy of the panic patient there are particular issues that need to be clarified and focused. The above vignette is illustrative of some of the points to explore and understand in the psychotherapy of the panic disorder patient. These include:

1. Clearly define and explore the meaning of specific recent stresses in the life of the patient.
2. Encourage the patient not to be afraid of his feelings.
3. Deal with issues of dependence/independence; responsibility and assertiveness.
4. Explore the concept of "emotional needs."
5. Help the patient obtain insight by dealing with the conflict within.
6. Guide the patient toward a more independent and responsible life-style.

Recent Stress

Stress plays an important role in the etiology of panic disorder. The majority of panic disorder patients have experienced an unusually stressful life event not long before their first panic attack. These stressful events can include both negative and positive changes, such as a geographical move, divorce or breakup in a

relationship, birth or loss of a child, or being laid off or
promoted at work. As mentioned previously, the panic-
prone patient is particularly vulnerable to stress.

Joyce was very specific about her recent stress and
her recent losses. She was struggling to keep her head
above water emotionally because she felt she now had
to take care of everything, had no (emotional) support
from her new husband, and had lost two islands of
security when her first husband remarried and her parents moved.

She had started a new job soon after her new marriage. She saw it as an additional burden where she had
to again prove herself and deal with the pressures of
sales quotas. She felt very inadequate. She saw herself
as having to stand alone emotionally for the first time.

The patient's stress must be understood on an individual basis. What may be stressful to one person may
not be an issue to another. The physician can help in
several ways. By offering acceptance and taking the patient seriously, the clinician allows the patient to relax
and start to work on his problems. By just being there as
an interested listener, the clinician can be a much
needed support person. By helping the patient gain insight and put issues in perspective, he can help quell
the individual's internal turmoil.

Dealing with Feelings

Anxiety is of crucial theoretical importance in psychoanalysis. According to this theory, "signal anxiety"
can serve the purpose of alerting the individual to internal danger, the result of unconscious conflict. Anxiety
represents fear of instinctual wishes, such as impulses,

emotions, and behaviors, that are socially unacceptable and consciously intolerable to the patient. The most usual issues involve sexual and aggressive impulses. Allowing these feelings to come to the surface and be expressed in the safe environment of therapy can be most helpful to the patient.

Emotional maturity has been defined as the ability to accept someone's anger and love as well as being able to tell someone that you love them or are angry with them. Many patients, although behaviorally mature and able to handle responsibility, show some deficit in their level of emotional maturity.

Joyce was brought up to be a "good" girl who followed the rules. She in turn received a total sense of protection and support. Her perfect world was shattered when her husband left her. She was filled with anger and rage. Except for occasional irritability and bouts of "spastic colon," these feelings went unspoken. In therapy, she was able to share some of her disappointment, hurt, and anger for the first time.

It soon became clear that she also resented having to go through the early phases of a new marriage for the second time. In her new relationship, she was afraid to give of herself completely because she felt vulnerable and was worried about being hurt. She was having difficulty talking to her husband. She was also filled with guilt over the fact that she had been brought up to believe that divorce was a taboo.

Independence/Dependence

Joyce was quite clear when she stated, "I always leaned on someone." On the one hand, she was upset that she no longer had her family to help her or stand behind her. On the other hand, she was conflicted over wanting control and yet wanting someone to share the responsibility.

Unlike Joyce, some panic patients are not aware of their need to lean on others for emotional security. In any case, it is important for the patient to understand that they are capable of standing on their own two feet psychologically. In most cases, they have been doing this anyway. It is often only a matter of adjusting to the psychological shift.

At the other end of the spectrum, much conflict can be stirred up when an overly independent person feels that they must ask others for help. This can be an issue when a mother goes out to work or when a worker is injured.

A helpful strategy is not to talk about dependency, but to refer to a *support system*. Patients need to learn that one can be dependent in a healthy way and that we all need to lean on others at times. This is not a sign of weakness.

Emotional Needs

All human beings have emotional needs. These include physiologic needs such as nourishment and rest, needs for self-esteem and affection, and spiritual needs. Intimacy, to love and be loved, has also been identified as a basic human need. Various theories of personality have incorporated this concept.

Erich Fromm identified essential human needs that must be met if a person is to grow. One of Abraham Maslow's major contributions was his recognition of the hierarchical organization of needs according to their potency and primacy.[2] It is surprising how many independent people are completely unaware of having needs and see themselves as isolated islands. This can play a role in their unhappiness. Therapy can do much to define their unfulfilled needs and encourage them to reach out to others.

Joyce's two husbands were very different in personality style. She saw her first husband as strong, affectionate, a compulsive worker, and reliable. Her second marriage was to a man who was more casual, less driven at work, and more involved with hobbies and friends. However, he was not openly affectionate.

These differences left her feeling that her second husband was not accepting and could not make her happy. Gradually, in therapy, she was able to gain a perspective. She could see that her second husband did care for her and was there when she needed him.

When she actually began to share her feelings, she found that he could be empathetic. She began concentrating more on his positive attributes. She also stopped idealizing her first husband, whom she had known since adolescence. During this process, she started to look at some of his more negative characteristics. This helped balance the picture and promoted separation.

Dealing with Internal Conflict

Dynamic psychiatry believes that since multiple forces impinge upon the ego, intrapsychic conflict can occur. Instinctual impulses may be in conflict with one another, instinctual impulses may conflict with superego values. Superego values may be in conflict when a situation poses two different alternatives.

There can also be conflicts between environmental demands and all portions of the personality. Conflict causes discomfort and dysfunction. It is often resolved by excluding one of the conflicting elements from consciousness through the process of repression. Anxiety can be seen as related to failure of repression, resulting in disturbing thoughts or impulses approaching consciousness.[3]

Psychotherapy will help the patient understand himself more completely, analyze his emotional conflicts, and acquire insight. "Insight-oriented psychotherapy is of benefit in the treatment of panic disorder or agoraphobia. Treatment focuses on helping the patient understand the unconscious meaning of the anxiety, the symbolism of the avoided situation, the need to repress impulses, and the secondary gain of the symptoms. A restriction of early infantile and oedipal conflicts occurs which correlates with the resolution of current stresses."[4]

Joyce was conflicted in many areas. In therapy, she dealt with the question, "Who am I?" She had repressed her negative feelings. She struggled with wanting to be a responsible adult. Her overprotective background made her feel fearful, insecure, and emotionally naked when she ventured out on her own. She had always interpreted overprotectiveness as love and was having difficulty realizing that caring comes in many packages.

Toward a More Independent Life-Style

All theories of personality talk of helping the patient to achieve emotional growth. This involves guiding the patient toward a more independent and responsible life-style. Freudian psychoanalysis focuses on allowing the patient to function at the highest level of psychosexual development. Karen Horney speaks of releasing the "real self" with all its potential for healthy growth. Maslow's followers talk of "self-actualization."

Joyce gradually began to take risks. She shared her feelings with others. She confronted her parents by making some of her own decisions while visiting them. She stopped feeling guilty. She put the men in her life in perspective. She sought and obtained part-time employment. She was able to see herself more clearly as a responsible adult. Her self-esteem improved; her self-confidence grew. She felt closer to her new husband and more secure in their relationship. Best of all, as she stood firmly on her own two feet, her panic attacks stopped.

The above material only represents the very basics, the tip of the iceberg, involved in doing therapy with the panic disorder patient. It does not take into account the art of therapy nor the individual style of the clinician. We hope that you will use the above information as a beginning.

Learning to treat the panic patient successfully will take time. It will require that you blend the above information with your own therapeutic style and the individual needs of the patient. It is important to remember that "the same key will not open the locks of all doors, and the interviewer must accumulate a variety of 'skeleton keys' that may be helpful in gaining access to the patient's trust and willingness to discuss private feelings and fantasies."[5]

9

Other Mental Health Treatments

Anxious patients often rush in many directions to seek an explanation and "cure" for their uncomfortable feelings. They look for anything to get rid of their anguish, including fads and magic cures. Fortune-tellers and health food claims are not unheard of in this sphere. At times alcohol and street drugs will be tried by some. Various mental health treatments may also be explored as this month's answer to their problems. The panic disorder patient is particularly prone to these adventures because of the intensity of their symptoms and the overwhelming effect the disorder can have on their mental status and life-style.

As a clinician, you may often be asked your opinion of the therapeutic value of various interventions being considered by your patient. With this in mind, I offer the following cross-section of other mental health treatments that are at times suggested to people who suffer from panic disorder. Included here are several, such as stress reduction, including the behavioral techniques of deep muscle relaxation, biofeedback, and breathing retraining, group therapy, and hypnosis, which I would consider secondary or adjunctive treatments for panic disorder. I will also discuss behavioral exposure therapy often helpful with the secondary avoidance behavior found with panic attacks. Lastly, I will review another behavioral approach, cognitive therapy, considered by many to be a primary treatment for panic disorder.

Stress Reduction

A difficult situation, even for normal average people, has the potential for producing a stress reaction. Coping mechanisms fail when something in your world

causes a threat to life, a risk of injury, or a loss of security. Change and adjustment are part of life. Therefore the stress of life can affect us all.

However, the panic-prone patient is particularly
vulnerable to stress. In the life of these patients,
stressful experiences, particularly separation or loss,
can precipitate panic attacks. The simplistic notion of
stress, popular in the media today, can really be quite
complicated.

Hans Selye first used the word *stress* to refer to the
nonspecific response of the general adaptation syndrome. The human stress response has come to include
both the subjective emotional as well as the physiologic
response to life events. Definition is often a problem
and quite individualized. It is important to remember in
evaluating the meaning of events in a patient's life that
what may be stress-provoking to one person may not be
stressful to another.

In general, there are three basic alternatives to any
stress situation. These include doing something to
change the situation, getting out of the situation, or
changing yourself so as to live more comfortably with it.
More specifically, there are various behavioral and emotional strategies that you can use to reduce stress. (See
those mentioned in Chapter 7.)

Your expectations in a situation are also important.
It is not really a situation that causes stress, but rather
the way that a person deals with the problem. People
who value control over sharing their feelings are more
likely to show signs of stress. Panic-prone patients certainly can often be included here. Those who recognize
and accept their own limitations and take a problem-
solving approach to life will do better.

Relaxation Training

Relaxation training as an approach to stress management can take various forms. The first is concerned with simply teaching individuals how to relax, using variants of the method known as progressive relaxation, developed by Edmund Jacobson. I particularly like the deep muscle relaxation techniques that are available on audiocassette so that they may be used at home. The second general approach to relaxation training is through some version of meditation or yoga. A third method is self-hypnosis. I will discuss hypnosis below.

A fourth way to teach relaxation is through the use of biofeedback. This method uses electronic instruments that provide overt, easily recognized information on the state of muscle tension. Such feedback is used by the individual to learn to reduce tension.[1] Breathing retraining is another arousal-reduction technique that is taught to panic patients by those who feel that hyperventilation is important in its etiology. Patients here are taught to raise pCO_2 levels through bag rebreathing or breath holding. Any of these techniques can be helpful to the panic patient who needs to reduce or modify stress.

Stress management programs have become very popular in the United States as a way to deal with the stress response or "burnout." Some programs employ techniques such as relaxation response and a common-sense analysis of major stressors on one's life. However, "group stress management programs carried out over several sessions often naively assume that individuals can in what amounts to a behavioral-hygiene approach, simply eliminate many of the sources of stress by restructuring their lives . . . some of the programs seem to ignore what psychoanalysis has taught us about conflict and the deeper roots of behavior."[2]

Some of these relaxation techniques, although effective in increasing parasympathetic tone and inducing muscle relaxation, have limitations. They can be time-consuming and boring. The repetition required may not be put into practice. Often, they cannot be used at the time or place that the panic attacks occur, such as while driving or when out in a group.

Group Psychotherapy

Group psychotherapy started in America as a medical experiment in 1906, when J. H. Pratt, a Boston physician, held classes at home for tuberculosis patients. While receiving instructions on health care, the patients learned to cope with the emotional problems arising from the illness. During World War II, due to insufficient psychiatric manpower, the concept and practice of group therapy grew.[3] Group methods continued to grow in popularity.

During the last 20 years, it has become a general cultural phenomenon as it exploded in all directions. Reeducational groups made up of a homogeneous selection of patients who suffer from a specific common medical or psychiatric difficulty have become commonplace in the mental health landscape.

A therapeutic group experience can be helpful for the anxiety and panic disorder patient. Here they can share their experiences and problems and learn that they are not alone or "different." Here, they will feel less isolated and begin to realize that they have a specific, understandable syndrome and not a unique bizarre condition.

In group, they can experience a decrease of anxiety and obtain relief of guilt feelings. They can also achieve an increase in self-esteem, as they are taken seriously, perhaps for the first time. Group therapy can foster self-expression and ventilation, as well as better interpersonal relationships and communication.

A supportive group can do much to foster risk taking and assertiveness and encourage the growth and maturity of the personality. Initially, the more adventurous patients will take risks and be more active. They can serve as significant role models, encouraging others to follow. Groups can utilize each other for support for some of the exposure and behavioral exercises that will be discussed below. Groups can continue to practice long after the formal treatment program concludes. Friendships made here can continue to act as a support system to help maintain improvement.

My own group style is a combination of teaching communication skills and using the psychoanalytic frame of reference to examine the needs of the individual, as these emerge in response to the interaction of the group. Here panic patients are taught to look at their own and other's feelings, to listen to other people, to give feedback on how they feel, and to check out their assumptions. Through group membership work in building cohesiveness, the patient and the group gain strength. As they grapple with the fantasy that the therapist will cure them, the group member deals with their dependency needs.

Finally, the group process helps bring into focus transference and resistance phenomena that can be analyzed. Through this process, the panic patient can achieve creative change within him- or herself and in their relationship with others.

Hypnosis

Hypnosis is derived from the Greek word *hypnos*, meaning to sleep. It is an artificially induced trancelike state, or rather a heightened condition of concentration, in which the subject responds to the suggestions of a hypnotist. It can be used to change an undesirable behavior or to provide symptom relief. To some, it seems to offer an easy, attractive, even magic solution to many problems. At times, it is suggested as an answer to stop panic attacks.

Although it is seldom regarded as completely adequate alone, hypnosis can be helpful in two general situations. First, it can be used to increase a patient's responsiveness to suggestions. Thus it can help remove symptoms of conversion or dissociation (tics, hysterical paralysis or blindness, loss of voice, amnesia, and various sensory disturbances). It can also be used to treat habit disorders, such as insomnia, nail biting, overeating, and cigarette smoking.

It may also be helpful for pain reduction or relief, can even be used by some for anesthesia of a degree that would permit surgery, obstetrics, or dentistry. Other applications include its use for the control of persistent and intractable hiccuping, psychogenic vomiting, and anorexia nervosa.

Hypnosis can also be used as an aid in decreasing a patient's inability or unwillingness to discuss certain topics. It is helpful in psychotherapy when the patient is mute, shows marked blocking or has amnesia for a certain period of time. Hypnosis is sometimes used for legal purposes because it can intensify the memories of witnesses or victims of crimes. It seems to be more productive when the patient has little psychiatric sophistication and the therapist is viewed as being prestigious, powerful, and having a high status.

Although hypnosis can help increase communication, obtain information, and aid in suggestion, the therapeutic benefits of this procedure are often questionable or are short-lived. The use of hypnosis alone as therapy, for panic disorder or any other emotional disorder, has its limitations. *No suggestion that is given by a physician leaves a lasting impression.* Either the same symptoms will return or a substitute symptom will replace the old one, because the *cause* of the symptom remains repressed, and the basic personality problem remains untouched.

Certain other disadvantages exist. Everyone cannot be hypnotized to the necessary depth. Suspicious or paranoid patients usually avoid or resist efforts at hypnosis. Furthermore, the material that is uncovered in hypnosis may be fantasy rather than actual memory. The patient also may consider hypnosis as having magic qualities that are either threatening or reduce the motivation for other forms of therapeutic work. Fragile or depressed patients may be vulnerable if they have unrealistic expectations. Another disadvantage, particularly counter-therapeutic in panic disorder, is that the patient can become dependent upon the therapist instead of achieving personality growth or independence of functioning.

Clinicians should remember that hypnosis can be helpful in certain instances. It can be used to encourage relaxation, and for this reason self-hypnosis may have some adjunctive value in panic disorder. However, it is not a magic or quick cure. A person's mental status should be evaluated before this procedure is used. Hypnosis always should be used with good clinical judgment and a knowledge of the emotional state of the patient. Although hypnosis can be an aid in psychotherapy, the author does not feel that it can take the place of therapy or a true commitment to change.

Cognitive Therapy

Cognitive therapy derives from the conception that emotional disturbances frequently stem from specific, habitual errors in thinking (cognition). Its overall strategy is a blend of verbal procedures and behavioral modification techniques. They are designed to help patients to recognize, to test out, and to convert distorted conceptualizations and dysfunctional beliefs underlying these erroneous "automatic thoughts." By acting more realistically and adaptively in regard to here-and-now psychological and situational problems, the patient is expected to experience improvement in symptoms.

The cognitive model of anxiety disorders teaches that adaptive anxiety comes about when a person is concerned about the outcome of being vulnerable—namely, being hurt or killed—and consequently is impelled to withdraw. In pathological anxiety, there is a generalized and intensified sense of vulnerability and subsequent inclination toward self-defense or escape. The various anxiety syndromes may be considered as expressions of an excessive function or malfunction of a normal survival mechanism.

The anxious patient's perception of danger is incorrect or excessive and is based on false premises. The anxious patient constantly misperceives danger and is relatively insensitive to cues indicating safety. The effectiveness of these patients' reality testing seems to be impaired. Their thought content revolves around the notion of danger and how to deal with it. They are drawn to consider the most negative consequences.[4]

According to this theory, the key feature of panic disorder is the patient's catastrophic misinterpretation of bodily or mental sensations as a sign that some specific harmful event is happening. The sensations that are misinterpreted are mainly those that are involved in normal anxiety responses (e.g., palpitations, breathlessness, dizziness, etc.). These sensations are perceived as much more dangerous than they really are.

For instance, palpitations are interpreted as meaning that the healthy patient is having a heart attack. Those who experience dizziness are fearful of fainting. Other symptoms are taken to mean that the patient is dying, losing control, or going crazy.

A cognitive approach to panic[5] proposes that an internal or external trigger stimulus is perceived as a threat. A state of mild apprehension results. The state is accompanied by a wide range of anxiety-produced bodily sensations that are interpreted in a catastrophic fashion. A further increase in apprehension occurs which produces a further increase in body sensations and so on, round in a vicious circle that culminates in a panic attack.

First, verbal cognitive restructuring therapy for panic disorder points out the irrationality of these catastrophic thoughts, and encourages patients to replace them with rational counter-thoughts. This approach provides the patient with accurate information relating to the nature of anxiety and, especially, relating to various diseases and physical disorders.

Second, it sets up typical structured exercises to help the patients identify their beliefs, examine the available realistic evidence, and seek alternate possible explanations. Because these patients tend to overestimate the probability and possible consequences of events, they should be encouraged to appraise the worst possible scenario realistically.[6] For instance, they may be asked, "What is the worst thing that could happen?"

When they experience symptoms of discomfort, they are taught to identify the underlying thought and its stimulus. They then decide whether the thought is rational or irrational. If the latter applies, the irrational thoughts are replaced with rational counter-thoughts. For example, someone fearful of losing control replaces this thinking with the knowledge that this has *not* happened, in spite of many months of experiencing panic attacks, and that no panic disorder patient has *ever* exhibited this tendency, although many have experienced this *fear* at times.

Cognitive therapy may also be helpful with secondary avoidance behavior. Because most patients believe that panic attacks are dangerous events, they think that it is logical to avoid such situations. This therapy method aims at undoing this behavior by teaching the patient that the attacks, though frightening, are really harmless and self-limiting.

Education is an essential part of altering the faulty thought processes and interrupting the cycle. Those patients who clearly understand the mechanisms of their panic attacks and secondary agoraphobia and the absence of significant consequences will do better. These educative aspects of cognitive therapy are similar to the approaches I have discussed under reassurance and education.

Advocates of this therapy form feel that it not only alleviates the discomfort of the anxiety attack, but also provides the patient with coping tools that they can utilize throughout their lives. They point out that although medication can also relieve discomfort, it does not teach specific coping methods that can be used to face fearful situations.

Exposure Therapy

Behavioral modification therapy in the form of therapist-assisted in vivo exposure (flooding) and self-directed in vivo exposure (programmed practice) is an effective treatment for the agoraphobia or the secondary avoidance behaviors often associated with panic disorder. Exposure refers to a range of techniques that bring the individual into contact with the feared event repeatedly, until the perceived aversive consequence is eliminated. Exposure is a principle originally advocated by Freud.[7]

"Psychobiological models . . . that view panic disorder, in part, as a fear of somatic sensations point to the potential for treatment of this disorder by exposure to interoceptive [somatic] clues . . . a hierarchy of events [in this case, sensations] is developed ranging from the least frightening to the most frightening. The patient is then encouraged to encounter each of these in order . . . therapists must use their ingenuity to devise ways of producing these [somatic sensations] in a systematic fashion. Biologic challenge procedures, such as sodium lactate infusions or CO_2 inhalations, provide an excellent means of producing sensations."[6] These invasive procedures are impractical for the average clinician.

Behavioral therapy techniques, like the one mentioned above, are often limited because they are not cost-effective or easy for the average practitioner to administer. If a therapist accompanies a phobic patient during exposure sessions, it can be time-consuming and expensive. In spite of this, there are some individual practitioners, as well as clinics, specializing in this treatment. Some patients refuse exposure treatment because they are unwilling to tolerate its distressing confrontations.

In spite of these limitations, studies are demonstrating that cognitive-behavioral techniques can produce total cessation of panic attacks in over 80 percent of panic disorder patients.[8] Data suggest that the use of behavioral, in vivo exposure-based treatment for agoraphobia produces stable results.

We are just beginning to learn about the long-term results of chemotherapy versus behavioral therapy for the treatment of panic disorder. The relative compared merits of behavioral therapy versus chemotherapy in reference to efficacy, safety, and patient acceptance is an area of interest and controversy. "Several studies have compared them but, because of design complexities and methodologic shortcomings, they are difficult to interpret."[9] Additional studies are needed.

"It appears clear that the use of combined behavioral and medication treatment generally results in a greater overall level of improvement and more rapid improvement, and promotes greater maintenance of improvement than the use of either treatment alone."[10] Studies in which the two have been used in combination for agoraphobia suggest that their effects are additive. Telch et al.[11] found that the combination of imipramine and behavior therapy is superior to either one alone.

Mavissakalian et al.[12] observed greater improvement among agoraphobic patients who received programmed practice and imipramine than among those who received imipramine alone. This same group did a more recent controlled prospective study of 62 patients over a two-year period.[13] Only 25 of the 62 patients completed the two-year follow-up. Two-thirds of this number no longer suffered from agoraphobia two years after treatment. The researchers suggest that imipramine and the therapist-assisted exposure sessions were most responsible for the positive results and most likely to provide consistent long-term maintenance results.

These various stress-reduction techniques and behavioral therapies can be helpful in reducing the fear and anxiety that is so distressing to panic patients. Group therapy, particularly, can add the dimensions of allowing patients to realize that they are not alone, while offering much-needed support. Exposure therapy is particularly helpful with agoraphobia, a secondary avoidance behavior, which often develops in panic disorder patients.

Although this author does not predominantly recommend any of these therapies as a primary or exclusive way to treat panic disorder, he does espouse an eclectic approach to treatment. It is felt that *the patient should be offered every possible therapeutic chance for success.* For this reason, these techniques are presented, so that they can be used, in whole or in part, when useful and necessary to aid you in your efforts to treat this difficult and complex disorder.

10

Treatment
Psychopharmacology

Training in psychiatry before the 1950s predominantly had a psychological or behavioral focus. Modern pharmacological discoveries in the last 35 years have created significant changes in psychiatric treatment. The introduction of major tranquilizers in 1952 with the discovery of chlorpromazine (Thorazine) greatly influenced the treatment of psychoses. In that same year, iproniazid (Marsilid), an MAO inhibitor, first used in the treatment of tuberculosis, was found to have antidepressant properties. The field soon widened to include compounds with antidepressant properties unrelated to the MAO inhibitors.

In 1961, chlordiazepoxide (Librium) ushered in the era of benzodiazepines. The increase in compounds to treat mental illness after this caused *Time* magazine in the early 1970s to proclaim on one of its covers that the twentieth century was the era of pharmacology. The 1980s brought with it new research information in psychopharmacology, particularly in the area of anxiety and panic disorder. The initial discovery that tricyclic antidepressants[1] and monoamine oxidase inhibitors[2] block panic attacks was met with skepticism by clinicians who held tight to earlier models of treatment.

However, as you have seen in prior chapters, these discoveries and subsequent neurobiological research have brought about several reclassifications of anxiety since 1980. In this process, panic disorder separated from generalized anxiety to emerge as a separate diagnostic entity. These changes refocused our attention on somatic symptoms, resulted in the reevaluation of treatment modalities, and began a new era in our ability to treat patients suffering from panic disorder. Various pharmacologic agents now have a firmly established place in treatment of this disorder. In fact, specific chemotherapy remains an important aspect of treatment in panic disorder.

There are now three classes of compounds with demonstrated efficacy for the treatment of panic attacks. These include tricyclic antidepressants, monoamine oxidase inhibitors, and the triazolobenzodiazepine, alprazolam. Other compounds are being researched in this area and show promise. This chapter will review the current status of the psychopharmacology of panic disorder and make some clinical suggestions concerning their use.

Beta Blocking Agents

Beta-adrenergic blocking agents, known to reduce heart rate and lower blood pressure, can also block the sympathetic effects of emotions. Granville-Grossman and Turner's demonstration of an antianxiety effect of propranolol hydrochloride (Inderal)[3] led to the speculation that beta blockers might reduce or eliminate the sympathetic discharge associated with panic attacks.

Tyrer and Lader[4] suggested that beta-blocking drugs may be effective in patients with predominantly somatic symptoms. Goodman and Gillman[5] specifically indicate that "propranolol is effective in controlling acute panic symptoms in individuals who are required to perform in public or in other anxiety-provoking situations . . ." (such as public speakers, actors, and musicians).

"A central mechanism of action has been suggested to explain the beneficial effects of propranolol in various anxiety states . . ."[5] However, others feel that a peripheral block of symptoms, which tend to reinforce the anxiety, appears to be the most likely mechanism.[6] Perhaps beta blockers can be helpful with the peripheral physical symptoms of anxiety, such as tremor, palpitations, and other evidence of increased sympathetic activity. Propranolol is not effective in anxiety where somatic symptoms are not significant. It has no direct effect on the psychic symptoms of anxiety. "Controlled studies have not supported its usefulness in panic disorder."[7]

The usual dosage for anxiety and panic is 10–30 mg up to four times per day. The oral dose should be given before meals and at bedtime. Administration with food delays peak plasma level time. However, nervous system side effects reflecting the central activity of propranolol can be prominent. These adverse reactions can include drowsiness, insomnia, trouble thinking, memory difficulty, and depression.[8] Propranolol is contraindicated for concurrent use or within two weeks of adrenergic-augmenting psychotropic drugs, including monoamine oxidase inhibitors.

Alpha-Adrenergic Agonists

Clonidine hydrochloride (Catapres) is an antihypertensive agent that possesses primarily alpha-2-adrenergic properties. It owes its antihypertensive effect to a predominant action on the central nervous system, where it apparently produces a decrease in the sympathetic outflow from the brain. Clonidine has also been proposed as a treatment for panic disorder. However, although it may block panic attacks, symptoms break through in a matter of weeks.[9]

Also, the dosage required (as much as 1.0 mg/day)

may cause side effects such as sedation, dizziness, and light-headedness. CNS side effects include nightmares, insomnia, restlessness, anxiety, and depression. Sudden withdrawal of clonidine may produce a hypertensive crisis.

Antidepressants

Tricyclic Antidepressants

Tricyclic antidepressants such as imipramine HCl (SK-Pramine, Tofranil, et al.) and desipramine HCl (Norpramine, Pertofrane) have shown good results. Imipramine has been studied most intensively. Six double-blind, placebo-controlled trials have been conducted as well as clinical open trials.[10] It has been shown to be effective in reducing both panic attacks and associated avoidance behavior.[11]

Anecdotal clinical reports suggest that a variety of other antidepressants are also effective, including nortriptyline, doxepin, amitriptyline, and fluoxetine. Clomipramine has been shown to be effective in panic disorder, but it is not yet available in the United States.[7] Neither the heterocyclic amoxapine (Ascendin) nor the monocyclic drug bupropion appear to be effective in a controlled trial.[12]

One clinical drawback of the use of tricyclic antidepressants in the treatment of panic disorder is that they will often block only the panic attacks and not alleviate the anticipatory anxiety or block generalized anxiety between attacks. As with depression, they require 3 to 6 weeks for maximum benefit. However, in my practice, I have seen initial improvement of panic symptoms even after one week.

There are two areas of controversy in the use of tricyclic antidepressants for the treatment of panic. These involve dosage recommendations and the concomitant use of behavioral therapy for secondary avoidance behavior. Because many panic patients are particularly sensitive to medication side effects, some clinicians recommend starting with the lowest possible dose, such as 10 mg/day, and gradually increasing the dosage by 10 mg every one to three days after that. They reason that this will avoid "the jitteriness syndrome."[13]

This is the initial temporary increase in motor restless, nervousness and anxiety, shakiness, tachycardia, insomnia, and "speedy" feeling experienced by about 15 percent of panic patients when started on tricyclic antidepressants.[14] Although this syndrome usually only occurs during the first week and dissipates with continued treatment, it can be a factor in compliance, patient cooperation with dosage increases, and can affect the dropout rate.

However, it has always been my contention that the moderate antidepressant outpatient dosage of 100–200 mg/day is usually needed for maximum benefit. Research on dose-response relationships would seem to confirm this. Ballenger and colleagues'[15] carefully conducted study utilized two groups with stratified plasma levels of 100 to 150 ng/ml and 200 to 250 ng/ml. Both groups did well.

Mavissakalian and Perel[16] reported that patients treated with imipramine have a significantly higher rate of response on doses greater than 150 mg/day. Zitrin et al.[17] have recommended that although some patients may respond to low doses of imipramine, most require 150–200 mg/day, and some may require doses of 200–300 mg/day. Lydiard[18] reported that patients receiving desipramine for panic who had plasma levels greater than 125 ng/ml fared significantly better than those with lower steady-state plasma levels.

The second area of controversy involves the combined use of behavioral therapy and chemotherapy. Most of the clinical trials using imipramine have used some sort of concomitant behavioral treatments because, traditionally, it was advocated that tricyclic antidepressants would block panic attacks; but avoidance behavior would not change without behavioral therapy.

Mavissakalian and colleagues treated agoraphobic patients with imipramine alone and a second group with imipramine and self-exposure. They observed little difference between the two groups, although there was some evidence favoring combined treatment. Garakani et al.[19] treated eight patients with panic disorder with imipramine alone and found the medication effective in six cases.

Anticholinergic and hypotensive side effects can be a problem. Panic patients are already overly tuned into their somatic symptoms, and are often very sensitive to medication side effects. They will therefore require vigorous education and support to keep them from worrying and remaining on their medication if these effects should occur.

Tricyclic antidepressants should be avoided if there is a history of acute angle glaucoma, significant prostatic hypertrophy, or cardiac conduction defects. Systematic data on the optimal length of treatment with tricyclic antidepressants are currently available. "In general, six months to a year of controlled symptoms and optimal functioning are desirable prior to initiating a taper of the medication."[7]

Monoamine Oxidase Inhibitors (MAOI)

Monoamine oxidase inhibitors (MAOI), such as phenelzine sulfate, have also been successful in blocking panic attacks. For some patients, they are better tolerated and more effective than tricyclic antidepressants. "There are now six placebo-controlled trials, five with phenelzine and one with iproniazid that have demonstrated their effectiveness."[10] Tyrer and colleagues reported that 65 to 70 percent of patients improved and maintained their improvement for months.[20]

In spite of these results, many physicians, including psychiatrists, are reluctant to use this group of medications. Many were taught that these drugs are dangerous (the initial MAOI, iproniazid, had to be discontinued, due to a large proportion of deaths from hepatocellular jaundice) and should be used only as a last resort.

MAOIs are still considered second-line agents by many because of possible toxicity and dietary limitations. However, this drug group is now considered safe if used properly. In light of their success in the treatment of panic disorder, physician attitudes will have to be reevaluated.

In the treatment of panic disorder with MAOIs, start at 15 mg/day and gradually increase to as high as 90 mg/day. The average dose of phenelzine is 45 mg/day. Maintain for six months and then taper. Many foods and drugs that exhibit indirect sympathomimesis need to be avoided. It is very important that patients be maintained on tyramine-free diets to prevent hypertensive episodes. Dietary restrictions include red wine, fava beans, broad bean pods and all spoiled, decayed, overripe, old, aged or fermented foods, especially proteins.

Drug prohibitions include ephedrine, phenylephrine, and phenylpropanolamine which are found in most cold or sinus medications, some nasal sprays, suppositories, stimulants and diet pills.[21] Reliable, compliant patients need to be chosen. If the patient adheres to the diet, side effects are limited to postural hypotension, occasional insomnia, and weight gain.

Tranquilizers

Logically, the benzodiazepines would seem to be appropriate for the treatment of panic disorder, an anxiety disorder. However, like the beta blockers, they do not reliably block panic attacks, and may only decrease the intensity of anxiety symptoms. The critical issue here may be affinity for the benzodiazepine receptor. Benzodiazepines may be useful as adjunctive therapy to decrease the intensity of anxiety symptoms, for instance, prior to the onset of the antidepressants. They may also be used to modify anticipatory anxiety. Although I prefer not to follow this practice, they are also offered by some physicians to patients to be used on a PRN or as-needed basis.

Alprazolam

One exception to not using benzodiazepines alone in the treatment of panic disorder and secondary avoidance behavior is the triazolobenzodiazepine, alprazolam (Xanax). This is the first benzodiazepine to be extensively and systematically studied. It has been indisputably shown in a large multicenter trial study to be an effective antipanic agent.[22] The FDA has not as yet approved alprazolam for use in panic and agoraphobia.

Alprazolam is particularly helpful in panic disorder because, unlike the antidepressants, it seems to alleviate anticipatory anxiety. This is a definite plus.

The dosage required for the treatment of panic disorder may have to be greater than the 4 mg/day maximum dosage recommended for generalized anxiety in the PDR.[23] Some patients may require a dosage of 6 to 10 mg/day. Ballenger has indicated that only about 20 percent of people need these higher dosages.[24]

This has also been the experience of this author. I usually start a patient on 0.75 mg to 1.5 mg daily dosage in divided doses, depending on the intensity of symptoms, frequency of attacks, and chronicity of the disorder. When an optimum therapeutic dose is reached, the regime should be continued for six to twelve months.[10,25]

The most common side effect with alprazolam is sedation. If this occurs, it will usually resolve in a few weeks. Other possible adverse reactions include ataxia, slurred speech, headache, and depression. As when taking any benzodiazepine, the patient should be told to avoid alcohol and other central nervous system depressants.

When the patient is functioning adequately, and you both feel confident that he can manage without medication, gradually reduce and then stop the dosage. As with other benzodiazepines, caution must be taken to avoid withdrawal seizures, particularly at higher dosages.

Patients should be advised not to stop alprazolam

suddenly. They should allow their physician to taper it gradually under supervision. A withdrawal rate of no more than 0.5 mg every half week had been recommended[26] when the daily dose is over 2 mg/day. More recent recommendations indicate a withdrawal rate of 0.5 every week for dosages over 2 mg/day. For dosages under 2 mg/day, reduce by 0.25 mg every week.

Because of its short duration of action, some patients treated with alprazolam may complain of feeling "nervous" or having anxiety between doses. Rebound can also be an issue upon the termination of treatment. Rebounding differs from withdrawal symptoms in that it is not the production of *new* symptoms, such as seizure, but a relative *worsening* of symptoms as compared with those which were present at baseline.

The issue of dependency is a question that often comes up in reference to the use of benzodiazepines such as alprazolam. Patient selection and patient education prior to the onset of treatment are important factors here. *Some people can become habituated or addicted to almost anything.* If your patient has a history of drug or alcohol abuse or questionable behaviors in reference to following therapeutic instructions, you should rule him out as a candidate for this class of medication.

At the time of initiation of chemotherapy, the patient should be given precise and firm instructions, along with appropriate explanation, of how you want him to take this medication. When questioned recently as to whether physicians should be concerned about aprazolam abuse, Ballenger indicated: "We haven't seen any cases of alprazolam abuse per se. We have seen it in the eight to ten percent of patients who abuse other things—alcohol, cocaine, and street drugs."[24]

Other Minor Tranquilizers

Other minor tranquilizers may also be helpful in the treatment of panic disorder. Early failures of the other benzodiazepines may be dose-related. However, in most cases, sufficient research material is not as yet available. Recent studies suggest that lorazepam (Ativan) may be effective and block panic attacks when given in sufficiently high doses.[27]

Clonazepam (Klonopin), a high-potency benzodiazepine, approved by the FDA for minor motor epilepsy, looks promising here. Studies show that it may be effective in blocking panic attacks.[28,29] An advantage of this longer-acting agent is that it may avoid interdose anxiety.

Buspirone HCl (BuSpar), a nonbenzodiazepine anxiolytic, effective in generalized anxiety disorder, is being studied in reference to panic disorder.[30,31] Its overall side effect profile shows minimal sedation, abuse potential, or adverse interaction with alcohol. It does seem possible that a subgroup of patients suffering from panic attacks and prominent symptoms of generalized anxiety may respond to buspirone.[7]

Relapse after Withdrawal of Medication

There is minimal research information on the percentage of patients who relapse when chemotherapy is discontinued. "There is general agreement that a substantial number of patients (approximately 30 to 70 percent) experience a return of symptoms within months after discontinuing medication treatment. However, I feel that this is where psychotherapy is important to deal with the stressors that helped precipitate the panic attacks.

When asked this question, I often compare it to the treatment of clinical depression. If an effective treatment response is achieved, and patients are maintained on medication for the suggested period of time, then this "bout" of panic should be obliterated. However, because panic patients most likely have an acquired or genetic physical vulnerability, this syndrome can be triggered again, at another time. As with depression, it may happen again in the future, if they are under excessive, and multiple, life stresses.

Clinical Choices and Guidelines

Little information exists as a guide to drug choice in the treatment of panic disorder. An individualized treatment plan is always needed. A clinician's rapport with the patient is paramount and cannot be minimized. The three most commonly used medications at this time are imipramine, phenelzine, and alprazolam. However, specific chemotherapy, combinations of agents, and dosage must be related to your experience and knowledge of your patient.

Klein prefers to start with a tricyclic antidepressant.[32] The antidepressants can be used first with patients who are significantly depressed as part of their clinical presentation, have a history of major affective disorder, or are secondarily depressed due to their panic attacks.

Alprazolam is the treatment of choice for many because of its being well tolerated. If a patient does not respond to an adequate therapeutic trial of the first medication, another should be tried. If both a tricyclic antidepressant and alprazolam are ineffective, an MAOI can be tried.

At times, combination therapy involving a tricyclic antidepressant and alprazolam may be necessary. This may be more effective and help keep the dosages of both medications low. A patient, for instance, with a secondary depression and panic disorder may also require both medications.

Regardless of which treatment approach you prefer, it is obvious that there have been tremendous and dramatic advances in our understanding of the pathophysiology and psychopharmacology of panic disorder. This has led to the development of various chemotherapeutic treatment strategies. Many unresolved questions remain. When answered, they will optimize pharmacological treatment. However, after many years of clinical confusion, therapeutic frustration, and unrelieved emotional pain, help is now available in the form of specific, effective medication to stop panic attacks. More advances are on the horizon. The future is bright.

11

Panic Disorder
The Future

The times are changing. There is quiet scientific revolution going on in psychiatry. Freud's classic, silent, black therapeutic screen is dissolving as voices sing the praises of a new biological focus in mental health disorders. In the forefront, leading the vanguard and representative of the foci of these changes, particularly in the anxiety disorders, is The Great Pretender, panic disorder. As we have seen, in our overview of panic disorder, research findings in physiology, genetics, and neurobiology have started to produce a new approach to mental illness in American psychiatry which has affected classification, diagnosis, differential diagnosis, and treatment.

The end result is that panic disorder, like the mythological Pan, long a hidden troublesome imp, is now more clearly seen and understood, and more effectively treated. The future will continue to bring more progress in all these areas as a kaleidoscope of research information interlocks to form a definite pattern of illuminated knowledge. Let us take a summary look at where we are and where we are going.

Classification

The new approach began with a change in psychiatric classification first seen almost a decade ago with the publication of the *Diagnostic and Statistical Manual-III*,[1] in 1980, by the American Psychiatric Association. Prior to this time, Freud's dynamic, analytical view, that psychic anxiety was primary and led to the development of physical symptoms, dominated psychiatric nosology. In the DSM-III, a more descriptive, empirical, and somatic approach is taken. Anxiety was now seen

as having both mental/psychic and somatic components. In this Manual of Mental Disorders, anxiety is
reclassified and panic disorder emerges as a separate
diagnostic entity.

Prior to this time, panic sufferers were diagnosed
as part of the overall category of generalized anxiety.
Now the syndrome has a separate name. By being seen
as a discrete condition, awareness spread, and some of
the clinical confusion surrounding this disorder began
to abate. During the last ten years, panic disorder has
become the most studied of the anxiety disorders. Although much new and helpful information is now available, many questions remain unanswered. Many new
areas of clinical interrelationship are beginning to surface or continue to be redefined. Our greater understanding of panic disorder has paralleled the general
explosion of recent research involving the brain and the
nervous system.

Etiology

Biological (Physical) Issues

Lewis Judd, director of the National Institute of
Mental Health, has stated that "ninety-five percent of
what we know about the brain has emerged during the
last decade."[2] "Because of the unprecedented expan-
sion in the knowledge of brain function during this decade, it has come to be known as the decade of the brain
or the decade of the neurosciences. . . . Molecular genetics is a major element of the scientific infrastructure
that is defining more clearly the nature of many neuropsychiatric disorders,"[3] including panic disorder.

In the 1971 special issue of *Medical World News* on Psychiatry,[4] editor Eli Robins stated:

> Only when we clarify precisely how the organism responds biochemically to the stresses that seem to produce the so-called functional disorders can we hope to arrive at specific therapies for those disorders . . . the stumbling block to understanding of the organism's response to the world around it is our ignorance of the biochemical bases of brain function. Once these are understood, the line separating "organic" and "functional" may disappear. . . . It is difficult to study the biochemical aspects of psychiatric illness. There are no animal models for any psychiatric illness, and extrapolating from animal data to human behavior is hazardous at best. In vivo chemical studies in humans are largely limited to analysis of body fluids—blood, urine, CSF. Because of the blood-brain barrier and other factors, it is usually impossible to determine whether alterations in fluid constituents reflect CNS changes.

Dr. Robins' words seems to represent the voice of the group. One can almost hear the frustration of the psychiatric community. It took at least fifteen years for real progress to be made. Positron emission tomography now permits examination of the chemistry of the brain in living human beings. The PET scan is a brain-imaging technique that safely provides quantitative regional measurements of biochemical and physiological processes. This information can be related to the mental functions of thinking, feeling, and behavior. In doing this, we can now investigate whether chemical and metabolic abnormalities within the brain might account for abnormal mental function and behavior.[5,6]

Such research has generated a dramatic shift in focus toward a biologic view of panic disorder. Specific biological correlates of panic disorder have been proposed involving various areas of the brain. These include the locus ceruleus. Stimulation here results in sympathetic arousal and an outpouring of catecholamines which leads to the physical symptoms of panic disorder.[7] Gamma-aminobutyric acid (GABA) opens up ion channels in neuronal membranes, causing hyperpolarization of the neurons and decreasing their excitability. This results in a decrease in anxiety.[8] Using PET scan techniques, recent researchers (which by coincidence included Dr. Robins) have identified a parahippocampal brain abnormality in panic disorder patients. Hypersensitivity here may determine vulnerability to panic attacks.[9]

If these abnormalities are persistent, they could be evaluated as genetic markers. As we have mentioned, studies have found that the disorder has a strong familial prevalence with rates in first-degree relatives reported to be as high as 30 percent.[10,11] There is evidence of vertical transmission from generation to generation[12] as well as greater concordance in monozygotic than in dizygotic twins.[13] The transmission pattern within families is consistent with single-locus genetics, and preliminary findings implicate the long arm of chromosome 16.[14]

These separate pieces are probably parts of a much larger puzzle that we may hope will be put together more fully in the future. If these abnormalities replicate, panic disorder may one day join pellagra, neurosyphilis, and other diseases with defined biologic correlates of the mental dysfunction.

Psychological (Emotional) Issues

The importance of stress and environmental factors in the etiology of panic attacks is still controversial. Although there is not a 1:1 correlation between panic attacks and stressors, many interesting and subtle relationships and some predisposing etiological factors have been seen. Patients with panic disorder are more likely than controls to have suffered adverse life events in the year prior to onset of symptoms.[15]

A recent study showed that patients with panic disorder had significantly more life changes. These events had a more adverse impact on them. Furthermore, the types of events experienced by the patients were more typically distressing than those experienced by the control subjects. The patients also reported events involving moves to other neighborhoods and/or cities far more frequently than did the control subjects.[16] Psychosocial information such as this certainly has implications for psychotherapy.

Differential Diagnosis: Relationship to Other Disorders

Depression

The relationship between panic disorder and depression remains unclear and controversial. Panic disorder seems to have component links to depression. Response to pharmacotherapy show that both respond to tricyclic antidepressant drugs, and neither responds well to the benzodiazepines, antianxiety drugs.

Epidemiological surveys and familial studies support the overlap between depression and panic disorder.[17,18] Some patients experience secondary depression, particularly if the panic and agoraphobia have become chronic. Longitudinal studies are needed to tell if panic disorder is a unique diagnostic entity or really an atypical depression. "The relationship between panic disorders and depression represents a model of the type of work that now needs to be done in understanding co-morbidity."[19]

Other Medical Conditions

Mitral Valve Prolapse. The relationship of panic disorder and the heart requires further investigation. "The incidence of mitral valve prolapse with panic attacks is greater than would be expected, but there is no evidence of a causal relationship. Most cardiologists agree that mitral valve prolapse by itself carries no increased risk of cardiovascular difficulty. However, the increased autonomic arousal associated with panic attacks and the occurrence of multiple episodes of anxiety and panic, may provide a risk factor for later development of arrhythmias and coronary artery disease. There is some evidence of an increased incidence of deaths due to cardiovascular disease among patients with panic disorders."[20]

Irritable Bowel Syndrome. As our knowledge and understanding of panic disorder, particularly of limited symptom attacks, grows, various clinical entities may come under the umbrella of this disorder. New connections will be made. For instance, a new area of interest in the diagnosis of panic disorder considers the question as to whether some irritable bowel syndromes are actually a form of panic disorder.

A recent study showed that both panic symptoms and gastrointestinal symptoms abated dramatically and rapidly after pharmacological treatment of the panic symptoms.[21] Additional studies showing similar correlations could have interesting implications for clinical practice.

Sexual Panic Attacks. Another new connection involves the work of Dr. Helen Singer Kaplan. She has brought a new dimension to the concept of panic with her interesting and innovative work on sexual panic states.[22] She points to the possible coexistence of sexual dysfunction and panic disorder. She has found a high coincidence of panic disorder and sexual phobias and aversions in her patients.

"The clinical features of persons who avoid sex are diverse. At one end of the spectrum are those who make love infrequently because they simply lack the desire. . . . At the other extreme are patients who actively and phobically avoid sex. These individuals have an intense aversive reaction. They feel disgust or revulsion in response to sexual stimulation. If they are unable to avoid sex, they may experience terrifying panic attacks with the accompanying autonomic nervous system symptoms. . . . We have found a high proportion of sexaphobic patients, from 25 to 50 percent depending on the criteria used, have underlying panic disorders . . ."[23]

These dual syndromes have provided an excellent vantage for studying the fascinating interplay between a presumably biological vulnerability to panic and the impact of cultural, neurotic, and relationship stressors. Kaplan found that "patients with underlying panic disorders tend to be extremely intolerant of separations and overly sensitive to rejections and criticism from their partners. These emotional vulnerabilities, as well as the patient's psychic defenses against them, are often material in the pathogenesis of their sexual and marital problems."[23]

In the past, patients with these combined syndromes involving sexual dysfunction and panic disorder showed a number of puzzling treatment failures. By noting the coexistence of these disorders, Kaplan has been able to make new inroads in treatment.

She found that her sexually phobic patients with underlying panic disorders were often too anxious and panicky to benefit from sex therapy. For this reason, she has been using medication known to block panic attacks with these patients. Her experience with the combined use of antipanic drugs and psychodynamically oriented sexual therapy has given her the opportunity to integrate biological and psychodynamic concepts of sexual anxiety and to develop comprehensive treatment strategies.

An Individualized Treatment Plan

The treatment of panic disorder continues to evolve. However, specific treatment is available. All clinicians, regardless of therapeutic persuasion, seen to agree on the value of *reassurance* and *education* of the patient. The value of psychotherapy is often debated and remains controversial. Some feel that psychodynamic or insight-oriented psychotherapy is ineffective in the treatment of panic disorder.[20] Others feel that it is of benefit in the treatment of panic disorder or agoraphobia.[24]

The doctor-patient relationship is a powerful therapeutic force. The issues of dependence/independence, separation/loss, and change/security may complicate recovery and are helpful to look at in psychotherapy. Stress, whether seen as an etiological factor and/or as a secondary complication, should be addressed in any treatment plan.

Others prefer a cognitive approach to panic. This behavioral model emphasizes conditioned responses that lead to the development of symptoms in accordance with classical learning theory. Here education of the patient is underlined and specific exercises are recommended to deal with the anxiety. Some add formal muscle relaxation techniques or meditation exercises to the regime.

Behavioral therapy, particularly in the form of exposure therapy, is effective against avoidance behavior. Critics of behavior therapy say that patients who improve are simply being taught to experience the attack as self-limiting and thus to avoid becoming disabled by their avoidance behavior, rather than actually experiencing a reduction or elimination of panic attacks and anticipatory anxiety.[25]

An important component of the treatment of panic disorder is pharmacologic. As we have noted, there are three classes of compounds with demonstrated efficacy for the treatment of panic attacks. These include tricyclic antidepressants, monoamine oxidase inhibitors, and the triazolobenzodiazepine, alprazolam. Other compounds are being researched in this area and show promise.

This book has underlined the importance of the medical evaluation, the psychiatric history, and the mental status examination in the differential diagnosis of panic disorder. After the diagnosis is made, this author's clinical preference involves an individualized treatment plan, including the aspects of reassurance

and education, chemotherapy, and individual psychotherapy. This is a psychiatric approach that works.

A new scientific, medical-model approach to anxiety patients is evolving in American psychiatry. Anxiety disorders are now seen as specific illnesses which
have precise diagnostic criteria, biologic correlates, and
effective treatment strategies.[26] This is particularly evident in this cluster of 13 characteristic physical and psychological symptoms that we call panic disorder.

A Holistic Point of View: A Psychological, Behavioral, Biological Synthesis

A neuropsychiatric focus has come to the fore during the last decade in reference to many emotional disorders, including panic disorder. "The brain is the
organ of psychiatry, and as we learn more about the
brain, we shall be better able to recognize its disturbances, treat its disorders, and prevent or contain the
dysfunctions it produces."[3] All aspects must be considered. René Descartes, the French philosopher, saw
mind and body as distinct entities, to be treated sepa-
rately. For many years, this dominated medical thinking. This is changing, as mind-body interactions are
being proven scientifically.

"The past ten years have witnessed an explosion of
research findings suggesting that the mind and body act
on each other in often remarkable ways . . . [for in-
stance] investigators are demonstrating that emotional
states can translate into altered responses in the im-
mune system . . . the two are joined by a 'feedback
loop' by which each influences the other [chemically].[27]
These hormonal interactions affect behavior and create

emotional symptoms. However, "our return to neuro-psychiatry will give due recognition to the behavioral, emotional, and cognitive aspects of brain functioning and not ignore one at the expense of another."[3]

This holistic approach is particularly important in the understanding of panic disorder, where psycho-social and biological factors show an extraordinary interrelationship. We have stressed this point of view throughout in reference to etiology, diagnosis, and treatment. As this book has pointed out, the future will probably show that a synthesis based on increased knowledge of psychological, behavioral, and biological forces will bring the picture of panic disorder clearly into focus. The 1980s has been a decade of discovery. The challenge for psychiatry in the 1990s is to clarify how these various factors interact in precipitating panic disorder and other psychiatric illnesses and to determine how different treatment modalities can be utilized, perhaps in combination, for effective clinical control.

References

Chapter 1

1. DaCosta JM: On irritable heart: A clinical study of a form of functional cardiac disorder and its consequences, *American Journal of Medical Sciences*, 1871:61:17–52.
2. Nemiah JC: Anxiety states (anxiety neuroses), in Kaplan HI, Sadock BJ (eds): *Comprehensive Textbook of Psychiatry*, ed 4, Baltimore, Williams & Wilkins, 1985, pp 883–894.
3. Goodwin DW: *Anxiety*, New York, Oxford University Press, 1986, p 10.
4. May R: *The Meaning of Anxiety*, New York, W W Norton, 1950.
5. Watson JB, Rayner R: Conditioned Emotional Reactions, *Journal of Experimental Psychology*, 1920:3:1–14.
6. *Encyclopedia of Psychology*, Eysenck HJ, Arbold W, Meili R (eds), New York, Continuum, 1982, pp 67–70.
7. Gregory I, Smeltzer DJ, Anxiety, somatoform and dissociative disorders (neurotic disorders), in *Psychiatry*, ed 2, Boston, Little, Brown, 1983, pp 285–300.
8. Cannon WB: *The Wisdom of the Human Body*, rev ed, New York, W W Norton, 1939.
9. Nemiah JC: Psychoneurotic disorders, in *The New Harvard Guide to Psychiatry*, Nicholi AM, Jr. (ed), Cambridge, Mass., The Belknap Press of Harvard University Press, 1988, pp 234–258.

10. Jenkins RL: *The Medical Significance of Anxiety*, Washington DC, The Biological Science Foundation, Ltd., 1955.
11. Laughlin HP: *The Neuroses in Clinical Practice*, Philadelphia, Saunders, 1956.
12. Anxiety: What causes it and how to treat it—A panel discussion, in *Medical Opinion*, Hackett TP, Cohen S, Kaufman E, O'Brien PA, Fisher S (panelists), 1977:6:5–25.
13. Rickels K, Schweizer EE: Diagnosis of anxiety disorders, in Primary Care Medicine, *Mental Health Adviser*, 1986:1:3–5.
14. *Diagnostic and Statistical Manual of Mental Disorders*, ed 3 (DSM-III), Washington DC, American Psychiatric Association, 1980.
15. Reiman EM, Raichle ME, Robins EE: The application of positron emission tomography to the study of panic disorder, *American Journal of Psychiatry*, 1986:143:469–471.

Chapter 2

1. Pascal B: *Lettres Provinciales*, 1656–1657, No. 127 (Condition de l'homme: Inconstance ennui, inquietude).
2. Freud S: Anxiety, in *A General Introduction to Psychoanalysis*, New York, Permabooks, 1958, pp. 400–418.
3. Nemiah JC: Anxiety states (anxiety neuroses), in Kaplan HI, Sadock BJ (eds): *Comprehensive Textbook of Psychiatry*, ed 4, Baltimore, Williams & Wilkins, 1985, pp 883–894.
4. Eaton MT, Peterson MH: Introduction to dynamic psychiatry, in *Psychiatry Medical Outline Series*, ed 2, New York, Medical Examination Publishing Co., 1969, pp 11–24.
5. Kramer M: Introduction—The history of the efforts to agree on an international classification of mental disorders, in *Diagnostic and Statistical Manual of Mental Disorders*, ed 2, Washington DC, American Psychiatric Association, 1968, pp xi–xviii.
6. Gregory I, Smeltzer DJ: Anxiety, somatoform and dissociative disorders (neurotic disorders), in *Psychiatry*, ed 2, Boston, Little, Brown, 1982, pp 285–300.
7. Sargant W: Drugs in the treatment of depression, *British Medical Journal* 1961:1:225–227.
8. Klein DF: Delineation of two drug-responsive anxiety syndromes, *Psychopharmacology*, 1964:5:397–408.

9. Schweizer E, Rickels K: Anxiety disorders: Overview, in *Proceedings: Anxiety Disorders: An International Update*, April 18–19,1985, Dusseldorf, Germany, Academy Professional Information Service, 1985.

10. Lewis A: Problems presented by the ambiguous word "anxiety" as used in psychopathology, *International Annals Psychiatry Rel. Discipl.* 1967:5:105–121.

11. Zal HM: Diagnosing and managing panic disorder, *Family Practice Recertification*, 1987:9: 99–114.

12. *Diagnostic and Statistical Manual of Mental Disorders*, ed 3 revised (DSM-III-R), Washington DC, American Psychiatric Association, 1987, pp 235–253, 422–423.

13. Zal HM: Panic disorder: Is it emotional or physical? *Psychiatric Annals*, 1987:17: 497–505.

14. Sheehan DV, Sheehan KH: The classification of phobic disorders, *International Journal Psychiatry Medicine*, 1983:12:243–266.

15. Rosenbaum JF: Limited-symptom panic attacks, *Psychosomatics*, 1987:28:407–412.

Chapter 3

1. Weissman M: Epidemiology of anxiety, in *Consequences of Anxiety*, a clinical monograph based on a symposium held October 8–11, 1987 in Orlando, Florida, Secaucus, New Jersey, Professional Postgraduate Services International, 1988, pp 5–6.

2. *Diagnostic and Statistical Manual of Mental Disorders,*ed 3 revised (DSM-III-R), Washington DC, American Psychiatric Association, 1987, pp 237–238.

3. Gorman JM, Liebowitz MR, Klein DF: Natural history: Panic disorder and agoraphobia, in *Current Concepts*, Kalamazoo, Michigan, a Scope publication, The Upjohn Company, 1984, pp 5–9.

4. Regier DA, Myers JM, Kramer M et al.: The NIMH epidemiologic catchment area program: Historical context, major objectives, and study population characteristics, *Archives General Psychiatry*, 1984:41: 934–941.

5. Weissman MM, Merikangas KR: The epidemiology of anxiety and panic disorders: An update, *The Journal of Clinical Psychiatry* (supplement) 1986:47: 11–17.

6. Goodwin DW: *Anxiety*, New York, Oxford University Press, 1986, pp 114, 116, 120.
7. Robins LN, Helzer JE, Weissman MM et al.: Lifetime prevalence of specific psychiatric disorders in three sites, *Archives General Psychiatry*, 1984:41:949–958.
8. Crowe RR, Noyes R, Pauls DL et al.: A family study of panic disorder, *Archives General Psychiatry*, 1983:40:1065–1069.
9. Noyes R, Clancy J, Hoenk PR et al.: Anxiety neuroses and physical illness, *Compr Psychiatry*, 1978:19:407–413.
10. Roy-Byrne P, Ashleigh E, Carr J: Personality and the anxiety disorders: A review of clinical findings, in *Handbook of Anxiety*, Roth M, Noyes R, Burrows G (eds), Amsterdam, Elsevier, in press, Volume 2.
11. Eubanks A, Hermenez D, Patterson W et al.: MMPI profiles in patients with panic disorder, presented at the 32nd annual meeting of the Academy of Psychosomatic Medicine, San Francisco CA, November 8, 1985.
12. Shear KM, Frances AJ: Panic disorder: Clinical presentation and evaluation, *Psychiatric Annals*, 1988:18:448–456.
13. Drossman DA: Irritable bowel syndrome: A multifactorial disorder, *Hospital Practice*, 1988:23:119–133.
14. Irritable bowel syndrome, in *Compendium of Patient Information*, Geffner ES (ed), New York, McGraw-Hill, 1988.
15. Marshall JR: Are some irritable bowel syndromes actually panic disorder? *Postgraduate Medicine*, 1988:83:206–209.
16. Lydiard RB, Laraia MT, Howell EF, et al.: Can panic disorder present as irritable bowel syndrome? *Journal Clinical Psychiatry*, 1986:47:470–473.
17. Young SJ, Alpers DD, Norland CC et al.: Psychiatric illness and the irritable bowel syndrome: Practical complications for the primary physician, *Gastroenterology*, 1976:70:162–166.
18. Liss JL, Alpers DH, Woodruff RA: The irritable colon syndrome and psychiatric illness, *Disorders Nervous System*, 1973:34:151–157.
19. Hallam RS: Panic-anxiety and alcohol dependence, in *Anxiety: Psychological Perspectives on Panic and Agoraphobia*, New York, Academic Press, 1985, pp 59–64.
20. Kanton W: Panic disorder and somatization, *The American Journal of Medicine*, 1984:77:101–106.
21. George DT, Ladenheim JA, Nutt, DJ: Effect of pregnancy on panic attacks, *American Journal of Psychiatry*, 1987:144:1078–1079.

Chapter 4

1. Zal HM: Panic disorder: An update, *Medical Times*,1988:116: 49–54.
2. *Diagnostic and Statistical Manual of Mental Disorders*, ed 3 revised (DSM-III-R), Washington DC, American Psychiatric Association, 1987, pp 235–253.
3. Kanton W, Vitaliano PP, Russo J et al.: Panic disorder: Spectrum of severity and somatization, *Journal Nerv Ment Dis*, 1984:175:12–19.
4. Boyd JH, Burke JD, Gruenberg E et al.: Exclusion criteria of DSM-III: A study of co-occurrence of hierarchy-free syndromes, *Archives General Psychiatry*, 1984:41:983–989.
5. Gorman JM, Liebowitz MR, Klein DE: Depression and panic disorder: Panic disorder and agoraphobia in *Current Concepts*, Kalamazoo, Michigan, a Scope Publication, the Upjohn Company, 1984, pp 14–16.
6. Lechman JF, Merikangas KR, Pauls DL et al.: Anxiety disorders and depression: Contradictions between family study data and DSM-III conventions, *American Journal Psychiatry*, 1983:140:880–882.
7. Thyer BA, Parrish RT, Curtis GC et al.: Ages of onset of DSM-III anxiety disorders, *Compr. Psychiatry*, 1985:26:113–122.
8. Zitrin CM, Klein DF, Woerner MG et al.: Treatment of phobias: I Comparison of imipramine hydrochloride and placebo, *Archives General Psychiatry*, 1983:40:125–138.
9. Liebowitz MR, Gorman JM, Fyer AJ et al.: Social phobia: Review of a neglected anxiety disorder, *Archives General Psychiatry*, 1985:42:729–736.
10. Lesser IM, Rubin, RT: Diagnostic considerations in panic disorders, *The Journal of Clinical Psychiatry*, 1986:47 (supplement):4–10.
11. Shear MK, Frances AJ: Panic disorder: Clinical presentation and evaluation, *Psychiatric Annals* 1988:18:448–456.
12. Barlow DH, Craska MG: The phenomenology of panic, in *Panic: Psychological Perspectives*, Rachman J, Mazer J (eds), Hillside, NJ, Erlbaum, 1988, pp 91–109.
13. Hauri P, Friedman M, Ravaris R et al.: Sleep in agoraphobia with panic attacks, in *Sleep Research*, Chafe MH, McGinty DJ, Walder-Jones R (eds), Los Angeles, Bis/Brs, 1985:14:128.
14. Messer JV: Anxiety and cardiovascular disease in the primary care setting, in Consequences of Anxiety: Management Strat-

egies for the Primary Care Physician, *Symposia Reporter*, a clinical monograph based on a symposium held October 8–11, 1987, Orlando, Florida, Secaucus, NJ, Professional Postgraduate Services International, 1987:11:11.

15. Mikerji V, Beitman BD, Alpert MA et al.: Panic disorder: A frequent occurrence in patients with chest pain and normal coronary arteries, *Angiology*, 1987:38:236–240.

16. Crowe RR: Mitral valve prolapse and panic disorder, *Psychiatric Clinics North America* 1985:8:63–71.

17. Raskin M, Peeke V, Dickman W et al.: Panic and generalized anxiety disorders: Developmental antecedents and precipitants, *Archives General Psychiatry* 1982:39:687–689.

18. Marshall JR: Hyperventilation syndrome in panic disorder—What's in the name? *Hospital Practice*, October 15, 1987, pp 105–118.

19. Raj A, Sheehan DV: Medical evaluation of panic disorder, *The Journal of Clinical Psychiatry*, 1987:48:309–313.

20. Roth M, Harper M: Temporal lobe epilepsy and the phobic anxiety–depersonalization syndrome. Part II: Practical and theoretical considerations, *Compr. Psychiatry*, 1962:3:215–226.

21. Cahill GF: Hypoglycemia, in *Scientific American Medicine*, Rubinstein E, Federman D (eds), New York, Scientific American, 1986: 9:1–6.

22. Stein MB: Panic disorder and medical illness, *Psychosomatics*, 1986:27:833–840.

Chapter 5

1. Pitts FN Jr, McClure JN Jr: Lactate metabolism in anxiety neurosis, *New England Journal of Medicine*, 1967:277:1328–1336.

2. Liebowitz MR, Fyer AJ, Gorman JM et al.: Lactate provocation of panic attacks: I. Clinical and behavioral findings, *Archives General Psychiatry*, 1984:41:764–770.

3. Katerndahl DA: Panic attacks—Psychologic response or medical illness? *Postgraduate Medicine*,1984:75:261–268.

4. Rifkin A, Siris S: Sodium lactate response as a model for panic disorder, *Trends in Neurosciences*, 1984:7:188–189.

5. Herman J, Deitch M: Understanding panic, *Rx Being Well*, 1986:4:33–36.

6. Boulenger JP, Unde TW, Wolff EA III et al.: Increased sensitivity to caffeine in patients with panic disorders: Preliminary evidence, *Archives General Psychiatry*, 1984:41:1067–1071.

7. Charney DS, Heninger GR, Breier A: Noradrenergic function in panic anxiety, *Archives General Psychiatry*, 1984:41:751–763.

8. Gorman JM, Askanazi J, Liebowitz MR et al.: Responses to hyperventilation in a group of patients with panic disorder, *American Journal Psychiatry*, 1984:141:857–861.

9. Liebowitz MR, Gorman JM, Fyer A et al.: Possible mechanisms for lactate's induction of panic, *American Journal Psychiatry*, 1986:143:495–502.

10. Klein DF: Panic disorders: Mitral valve prolapse, cardiorespiratory symptoms: Program overview, symposium, anxiety and depression: New concepts and therapeutic implications. Presented by the Department of Psychiatry and the Division of Continuing Mental Health Education of the Medical College of Pennsylvania, Philadelphia, June 29, 1983.

11. Shader RI, Goodman M, Genei J: Panic disorders: Current perspectives, *Journal Clinical Psychopharmacology*, 1982:2 (suppl 6):2–10.

12. Katon W: Panic disorder and somatization, *American Journal Medicine*, 1984:77:101–106.

13. Klein DF: Etiology and pathophysiology, symposium on anxiety, panic and phobic disorders held May 17, 1985, *Charter Quarterly Review*.

14. Ley R: Blood, breath, and fears: A hyperventilation theory of panic attacks and agoraphobia, *Clinical Psychological Review*, 1985:5:271–285.

15. Gorman JM, Askanazi J, Liebowitz MR et al.: Response to hyperventilation in a group of patients with panic disorder, *American Journal Psychiatry*, 1984:141:857–861.

16. Katerndahl DA: Panic, *American Family Physician*,1982:26:125–129.

17. Davis JM: Minor tranquilizers, sedatives and hypnotics, in *Comprehensive Textbook of Psychiatry/IV*, Kaplana HI, Sadock BJ (eds), ed 4, Baltimore, Williams & Wilkins, 1985, pp 1537–1553.

18. Raichle ME: Positron emission tomography, *Annu Rev Neurosci*, 1983:6:249–267.

19. Reiman EM, Raichle, ME, Robins E et al.: The application of positron emission tomography to the study of panic disorder, *American Journal Psychiatry*, 1986:143:469–471.

20. Klein DF, Rabkin JG (eds): *Anxiety: New Research and Changing Conceptions*, New York, Raven Press, 1981.
21. Crowe RR, Noyes R, Clancy J et al.: The familial prevalence of anxiety neurosis, *Archives General Psychiatry*, 1978:35:1057–1059.
22. Crowe RR, Noyes R, Pauls DL et al.: A family study of panic disorder, *Archives General Psychiatry*, 1983:40:1065–1069.
23. Torgersen S: Genetic factors in anxiety disorders, *Archives General Psychiatry*, 1983:40:1085–1089.
24. Surman OS, Sheehan DV, Fuller TC et al.: Panic disorder in genotypic HLA identical sibling pairs, *American Journal Psychiatry*, 1983:140:237–238.
25. Crowe, RR, Noyes R Jr., Wilson AF et al.: A linkage study of panic disorder, *Archives General Psychiatry*, 1987:44:933–937.

Chapter 6

1. Sheehan DV, Sheehan KE, Minichiello WE: Age of onset of phobic disorders: A reevaluation, *Compr Psychiatry*, 1981:22:544–553.
2. Crowe RR, Noyes R Jr, Pauls DR et al.: A family study of panic disorder, *Archives General Psychiatry*, 1983:40:1065–1069.
3. Shakespeare W, *The Tempest*, Act II, Scene I, Line 243.
4. Cowley DS, Roy-Byrne PP: Panic disorder: Psychosocial aspects, *Psychiatric Annals*, 1988:18:464–467.
5. Raskin M, Peeke V, Dickman W et al.: Panic and generalized anxiety disorders: Developmental antecedents and precipitants, *Archives General Psychiatry*,1982:39:687–689.
6. Rae-Grant Q: Disorders of childhood and adolescence, in *A Method of Psychiatry*, Grebon SE, Rakoff VM, Voineskos G (eds), ed 2, Philadelphia, Lea and Febiger, 1985, pp 270–290.
7. Weissman M, Epidemiology of anxiety, in *Consequences of Anxiety: Management Strategies for the Primary Care Physician*, a clinical monograph based on a symposium, October 8–11, 1987, Orlando, Florida, pp 5–6.
8. Gittelman R, Klein DR: Childhood separation anxiety and adult agoraphobia, in *Anxiety and Anxiety Disorders*, Tuma H, Moser J (eds), Hillsdale, NJ, Erlbaum, 1985.
9. Klerman GL: Current trends in clinical research on panic attacks, agoraphobia, and related anxiety disorders, *Journal Clinical Psychiatry* 1986:47 (supplement):37–39.

10. Kagan, J, Reznick JS, Snidman N: Biological bases of childhood shyness. *Science*, 1988:240:167–171.
11. Zal HM: Four stages of life: Part I, *Osteopathic Medical News*, 1988:5:28.
12. Blos P: *On Adolescence: A Psychoanalytic Interpretation*, New York, Free Press, 1962, pp 148–158.
13. Zal HM: Four stages of life: Part II, *Osteopathic Medical News*, 1988:5:21.
14. Robins CN, Helzer JE, Weissman MM et al.: Lifetime prevalence of specific psychiatric disorders in three sites, *Archives General Psychiatry*, 1984:41:949–958.

Chapter 7

1. Shear MK, Frances AJ: Panic disorder: Clinical presentation and evaluation, *Psychiatric Annals*, 1988:18:448–456.
2. Zal HM: Diagnosing and managing panic disorder, *Family Practice Recertification*, 1987:9:106.

Chapter 8

1. Wolberg LR, *The Technique of Psychotherapy*, ed 2, New York, Grune & Stratton, 1967, pp 3–11.
2. Thetford WN, Walsh R: Theories of personality and psychopathology: Schools derived from psychology and philosophy, in *Comprehensive Textbook of Psychiatry/IV*, Kaplan HI, Sadock BJ (eds), Baltimore, Williams & Wilkins, 1985, pp 459–481.
3. Eaton MJ, Peterson MH, *Psychiatry: Medical Outline Series*, ed 2, New York, Medical Examination Publishing Co., Inc., 1969, pp 11–23.
4. Kaplan HI, Sadock BJ, Panic disorder and agoraphobia, in *Clinical Psychiatry from Synopsis of Psychiatry*, Baltimore, Williams & Wilkins, 1988, pp 166–172.
5. Gregory I, Smeltzer DJ: *Psychiatry*, Boston, Little, Brown, 1983, p 37.

Chapter 9

1. Wilder JF, Plutchik R: Stress and psychiatry, in *Comprehensive Textbook of Psychiatry/IV*, Kaplan HI, Sadock BJ (eds), Baltimore, Williams & Wilkins, 1985, pp 1198–1203.
2. Rodgers MP, Reich P: Psychosomatic medicine and consultation-liaison psychiatry: The concept of stress, in *The New Harvard Guide to Psychiatry*, Nicholi AM Jr. (ed), Cambridge, Mass, The Belknap Press of Harvard University Press, 1988, pp 391–394.
3. Pollatin P: *A Guide to Treatment in Psychiatry*, Philadelphia, Lippincott, 1966, pp 100–115.
4. Beck AT: Cognitive therapy, in *Comprehensive Textbook of Psychiatry/IV*, Kaplan HI, Sadock BJ (eds), Baltimore, Williams & Wilkins, 1985, pp 1432–1438.
5. Clark DM: A cognitive approach to panic, *Behav Res Ther*, 1986:24: 461–470.
6. Rapee RM, Barlow DH: Panic disorder: Cognitive-behavioral treatment, *Psychiatric Annals*,1988:18:473–477.
7. Freud S: Turnings, in The ways of psychoanalytic therapy, in Sigmund Freud, *Collected Papers*, Volume 2, New York, Basic Books, 1959.
8. Beck AT: Cognitive approaches to panic disorder, in *Panic: Psychological Perspectives*, Rachman S, Maser JD (ed), Hillsdale, NJ, Erlbaum, 1988.
9. Noyes R, Chaudry DR, Domingo DV: Pharmacologic treatment of phobic disorders, *Journal Clinical Psychiatry*, 1986:47:445–452.
10. Lydiard RB: Panic disorder: Pharmacological treatment, *Psychiatric Annals*, 1988:18:468–472.
11. Telch MJ, Agras WS, Taylor CB et al.: Combined pharmacological and behavioral treatment for agoraphobia, *Behav Res Ther*, 1985:23:325–335.
12. Mavissakalian M, Michelson L, Dealy RS: Pharmacological treatment of agoraphobia: Imipramine versus imipramine with programmed practice, *British Journal Psychiatry*, 1983:143:348–355.
13. Mavissakalian M, Michelson L: Agoraphobia: Relative and combined effectiveness of therapist-assisted in vivo exposure and imipramine, 1986:143:1106–1112.

Chapter 10

1. Klein, DF: Delineation of two drug-responsive anxiety syndromes, *Psychopharmacologia*, 1964:53:397–408.
2. West ED, Dally PJ: Effects of iproniazid in depressive syndromes, *British Medical Journal*, 1959:1:1491–1494.
3. Granville-Grossman, KL, Turner, P: The effect of propranolol on anxiety, *Lancet*, 1966:1:788–790.
4. Tyrer, PJ, Lader, MH: Response to propranolol and diazepam in somatic anxiety, *British Medical Journal*, 1974:2:14–16.
5. *Goodman and Gilman's The Pharmacological Basis of Therapeutics*, Gilman, AG, Goodman, LS, Rall, TW, Murad, F, ed 71, New York, Macmillan, 1985, pp. 194–199.
6. Bonn JA, Turner P, Hicks DL: Beta-adrenergic receptor blockage with practolol in treatment of anxiety, *Lancet*, 1972:I:814–815.
7. Lydiard RB: Panic disorder: Pharmacological treatment, *Psychiatric Annals*, 1988:18:468–472.
8. Noyes R, Anderson DJ, Clancy J et al.: Diazepam and propranolol in panic disorder and agoraphobia, *Archives General Psychiatry*, 1984: 41:287–292.
9. Liebowitz MR, Fyer AJ, McGrath P et al.: Clonidine treatment of panic disorder, *Psychopharmacol Bulletin* 1981:17:122–123.
10. Ballenger, JC: Update on anxiety and panic disorders: Pharmacotherapy of the panic disorders, *The Journal of Clinical Psychiatry*, 1986:47:6 (supplement):27–32.
11. Mavissikalian M, Michelson L, Dealy RS: Pharmacological treatment of agoraphobia: Imipramine versus imipramine with programmed practice, *British Journal of Psychiatry*, 1983:143:348–355.
12. Sheehan DV, Davidson J, Manschreck T et al.: Lack of efficacy of a new antidepressant (Bupropion) in the treatment of panic disorder with phobias, *Journal Clin Psychopharmacol*, 1983:3:28–31.
13. Pohl R, Yeragani VK, Balon R et al.: The Jitteriness Syndrome in panic disorder patients treated with antidepressants, *Journal Clinical Psychiatry*, 1988:49:100–104.
14. Muskin PR, Fryer AJ: Treatment of panic disorder, *Journal Clinical Psychopharmacol*, 1981:1:81–90.
15. Ballenger JC, Peterson GA, Laraia M et al.: A study of plasma catecholamines in agoraphobia and the relationship of serum tricyclic levels to treatment response, in *Biology of Agoraphobia*, Ballenger, JC (ed.), Washington DC, APA Press, 1984.

16. Mavissakalian M, Perel J: Imipramine in the treatment of agoraphobia: Dose-response relationship, *American Journal Psychiatry*, 1985:142:1032–1036.

17. Zitrin CM, Klein DF, Woerner MG: Behavior therapy, supportive psychotherapy, imipramine, and phobias, *Archives General Psychiatry*, 1978:35:307–316.

18. Lydiard RB: Desipramine in agoraphobia with panic attacks: An open, fixed-dose study, *Journal Clinical Psychopharmacol*, 1987:7:258–260.

19. Garakani H, Zitrin CM, Klein DF: Treatment of panic disorder with imipramine alone, *American Journal Psychiatry*, 1984:141:446–448.

20. Tyrer P, Candey J, Kelly D: A study of the clinical effects of phenelzine and placeba in the treatment of phobic anxiety, *Psychopharmacologia*, 1973:32:237–254.

21. Zisook S: A clinical overview of monoamine oxidase inhibitors, *Psychosomatics*, 1985:26:240–251.

22. Ballenger JC, Burrows GD, DuPont R et al.: Alprazolam in panic disorder and agoraphobia: Results from a multicenter trial. I. Efficacy in short-term treatment, *Archives General Psychiatry*, 1988:45:413–422.

23. Schatzberg AF: Panic disorder, *Medicine and Psychiatry*, 1985:2:2.

24. Dwyer BJ: Experts update management of phobias, panic disorder, *The Psychiatric Times/Medicine and Behavior*, February 1988, pp. 34–36.

25. Sheehan DV: Current perspectives in the treatment of panic and phobic disorders, *Drug Therapy*, September 1982, pp. 179–191.

26. Gonzalez ER: Panic disorder may respond to new antidepressants, *Journal American Medical Association*, 1982:248:3077–3086.

27. Charney DS, Woods SW, Goodman WK et al.: The efficacy of lorazepam in panic disorders, presented at the 140th Annual Meeting of the American Psychiatric Association, Chicago, Ill., May 1987.

28. Spier SA, Tesar GE, Rosenbaum JF et al.: Treatment of panic disorder and agoraphobia with clonazepam, *Journal Clinical Psychiatry*, 1986:47:238–242.

29. Tesar GE, Rosenbaum JF, Pollack MH et al.: Clonazepam versus alprazolam in the treatment of panic disorder: Interim analysis of data from a prospective, double-blind, placebo-controlled trial, *Journal Clinical Psychiatry*, 1987:48 (supplement):16–21.

30. Robinson D: Update on the treatment of panic disorder: Non-benzodiazepine anxiolytics, including buspirone. Presented at the annual ACDEU Meeting, Key Biscayne, Florida, May 31–June 3, 1988.
31. Personal communication with Ted Donosky, MD, Associate Director, Pharmaceutical Medical Services, Mead Johnson Pharmaceuticals, Evansville, Indiana, October 7, 1988.
32. Klein DF: "Latest Developments in the Treatment of Anxiety and Panic Disorders," lecture at Philadelphia Psychiatric Center, Philadelphia, PA, Tuesday, March 10, 1987.

Chapter 11

1. *Diagnostic and Statistical Manual of Mental Disorders*, ed 3 (DSM-III), Washington DC, American Psychiatric Association, 1980.
2. Detzen J: Opening the windows of the mind, *The Philadelphia Inquirer*, October 18, 1988, p 1E.
3. Staff: Emphasis on brain takes psychiatry on exciting path, *Psychiatric News*, August 5, 1988:12(15):5.
4. Robins E: Introduction, Chemical theories and mental illness, *Medical World News: Psychiatry 1971*, New York, McGraw-Hill, 1971, pp 7–21.
5. Raichle ME: Positron emission tomography, *Annual Rev Neurosci* 1983:6:249–267.
6. Jacobson HG (section ed), Positron emission tomography—A new approach to brain chemistry, *Journal American Medical Association*, 1988:260(18):2702–2710.
7. Redmond DE: Alterations in the function of the nucleus locus coeruleus: A possible model of four studies of anxiety, in *Animal Studies in Psychiatry and Neurology*, Hanin I, Usdin E (eds), New York, Pergamon Press, 1987.
8. Paul SM, Skolnick P: Benzodiazepine receptors and psychopathological states: Towards the neurobiology of anxiety, in *Anxiety: New Research and Changing Concepts*, Klein DF, Rabkin JG (eds), New York, Raven Press, 1981.
9. Reiman EM, Raichle ME, Robbins E et al.: The application of positron emission tomography in the study of panic disorder, *American Journal Psychiatry*, 1986:143:469–471.

10. Crowe RR, Noyes R, Clancy J et al.: The familial prevalence of anxiety neurosis, *Archives General Psychiatry*, 1978:35:1057–1059.
11. Crowe RR, Noyes R, Pauls DL et al.: A family study of panic disorder, *Archives General Psychiatry*, 1983:40:1065–1069.
12. Pauls DL, Bucher KD, Crowe RR et al.: A genetic study of panic disorder pedigrees, *American Journal Human Genetics*, 1980:32:639–644.
13. Torgersen S: Genetic factors in anxiety disorders, *Archives General Psychiatry*, 1983:40:1085–1089.
14. Crowe RR, Noyes R Jr., Wilson AF et al.: A linkage study of panic disorder, *Archives General Psychiatry*, 1987:44:933–937.
15. Faravelli C: Life events preceding the onset of panic disorder, *Journal Affective Disorders*, 1985:9:103–105.
16. Roy-Bryne P, Geraci M, Unde T: Life events and the onset of panic disorder, *American Journal Psychiatry* 1986:143:1424–1427.
17. Pauls DL, Noyes R, Crowe RR: The familial prevalence in second-degree relatives of patients with anxiety neurosis (panic disorder), *Journal Affective Disorders*, 1979:1:279–285.
18. Leckman JF, Weissman MM, Merikanges, KR et al.: Panic disorder and major depression: Increased risk of depression, alcoholism, panic and phobic disorders in families of depressed probands with panic disorder, *Archives General Psychiatry*, 1983:40:1055–1060.
19. Kupfer DJ: Introduction: New directions in biologic psychiatry, *Journal Clinical Psychiatry*, 1986:47:10 (supplement):3–5.
20. Klerman GL: Current trends in clinical research on panic attacks, agoraphobia and related anxiety disorders, *Journal Clinical Psychiatry*, 1986:47:6 (supplement): 37–39.
21. Lydiard BR, Laraia MT, Howell EF et al.: Can panic disorder present as irritable bowel syndrome? *Journal Clinical Psychiatry*, 1986:47:470–473.
22. Kaplan HS: *Sexual Aversion, Sexual Phobias, and Panic Disorder*, New York, Brunner/Mazel, 1987, pp 3–150.
23. Kaplan HS: Sexual panic attacks, *Psychiatric Times*, 1988:5:1 & 20.
24. Kaplan HI, Sadock BJ: Panic disorder and agoraphobia, *Clinical Psychiatry*, Baltimore, Williams & Wilkins, 1988, pp 166–172.
25. Nemiah J: Anxiety and psychodynamic theory in *Psychiatry Update*, Grinspoon L (ed), Volume 3, Washington DC, American Psychiatric Press, 1984.

26. McGlynn TJ, Metcalf HL (eds): *Diagnosis and Treatment of Anxiety Disorders: A Physician's Handbook,* American Psychiatric Press, 1989, p vii.
27. Gelman D, Hager M: Body and Soul, *Newsweek,* November 7, 1988, pp 88–97.

Index

About the Author

H. Michael Zal, D.O., F.A.C.N., is a Board-Certified Psychiatrist who maintains a full-time private practice in Bala Cynwyd, Pennsylvania. He is a clinical professor in the Department of Psychiatry at the Philadelphia College of Osteopathic Medicine and chairman of the Psychiatric Service at Metropolitan Hospital–Central Division, Philadelphia. Dr. Zal is a Fellow of the American College of Neuropsychiatrists and a member of the University of Pennsylvania Private Practice Research Group. He is associated with the Philadelphia Psychiatric Center and the Charter–Fairmount Institute, Philadelphia, Pennsylvania.

Dr. Zal was the producer/host of a cable television show, "Mental Notes with Dr. Michael Zal," for American Cablevision of Pennsylvania from 1982 to 1985. The show won two awards for excellence in community broadcasting.

He is a lecturer on mental health topics and a medical writer with numerous published articles. He was the winner of the 1988 Eric W. Martin Memorial Award, presented by the American Medical Writers Association, for outstanding writing on a topic related to therapeutics or the pharmaceutical sciences. His winning article, Panic disorder: Is it emotional or physical?, was published in the July, 1987, issue of Psychiatric Annals.

Dr. Zal is a member of the editorial board of Osteopathic Annals and an editorial consultant in psychiatry for the Journal of the American Osteopathic Association and the American College of Neuropsychiatrists.